OFFICER EFFICIENCY REPORT

SECTION I

1. LAST NAME - FIRST NAME - INITIAL	2. SERVICE NUMBER	3. GRADE	4. CONTROL BRANCH	5. COMPONENT
MUCKERMAN, JOSEPH E., JR.	O 59 356	1st Lt	Arty	RA

6. UNIT, ORGANIZATION AND STATION	7. PERIOD OF REPORT FROM	TO	8. DAYS OF DUTY	LEAVE	OTHER
BTRY B, 37th AAA Gun Bn, APO 503, FEC	7 Nov 51	8 May 52	184	0	0

9. NAME, GRADE, SERVICE NUMBER AND ORGANIZATION OR UNIT OF RATING OFFICER
ARTHUR J DICK, Captain, 01081646
BTRY B, 37th AAA Gun Bn. APO 503, FEC

10. NAME, GRADE, SERVICE NUMBER AND ORGANIZATION OR UNIT OF INDORSING OFFICER
RALPH G. DUNCAN, Major 0325842
Hqs, 37th AAA Gun Bn. APO 503, FEC

11. REASON FOR REPORT PCS RATED OFFICER [ ] CHANGE DUTY RATED OFFICER [X] OTHER *(Specify)*
(SEMI) ANNUAL [ ] PCS RATING OFFICER [ ] CHANGE DUTY RATING OFFICER [ ]

12.

(Do not write in this space)

13. DUTIES ACTUALLY PERFORMED ON PRESENT JOB *(Give his duty MOS* 1172 *, assignment, and briefly describe major additional duties)* Range Platoon Officer, Executive Officer, Communications Officer, Troop Information Officer, Training Officer

14. ENTRIES ARE BASED ON
OBSERVATION OF 30-59 DUTY DAYS [ ] OBSERVATION OF 60 DUTY DAYS OR MORE [X] OFFICIAL REPORTS [ ]

15. DESCRIPTION OF OFFICER RATED AND COMMENTS *(These paragraphs should cover physical, mental, moral qualities of rated officer, and any special strengths or weaknesses affecting his ability to do certain assignments not covered elsewhere in the report)*

A. COMMENTS OF RATING OFFICER

Physically, mentally and morally this officer is of the highest caliber. He is an asset and a credit to the service. When duty required extra long hours he performed all his duties consciously, efficiently and in a cheerful manner. His manner of utilizing manpower is superior. He is a strong leader of men. He sets an example to those under him which results in mass co-operation and willingness of all personnel striving to do their best work. I would be happy to have him serve with me at any time.

B. COMMENTS OF INDORSING OFFICER [ ] I DO NOT KNOW THE RATED OFFICER BUT I HAVE CONFIDENCE IN THE RATER'S JUDGMENT
[ ] I DO NOT KNOW THE RATED OFFICER VERY WELL BUT I HAVE CONFIDENCE IN THE RATER'S JUDGMENT

16A. **RATER'S CERTIFICATE**

I CERTIFY THAT TO THE BEST OF MY KNOWLEDGE AND BELIEF ALL ENTRIES MADE HEREON BY ME ARE TRUE AND IMPARTIAL AND ARE IN ACCORDANCE WITH AR 600-185.

DATE | SIGNATURE OF RATER

OFFICIAL RELATION TO RATED OFFICER CO of an AAA Gun Btry in which he serves as Range Plat Ldr.

B. **INDORSER'S CERTIFICATE**

I CERTIFY THAT TO THE BEST OF MY KNOWLEDGE AND BELIEF ALL ENTRIES MADE HEREON BY ME ARE TRUE AND IMPARTIAL AND ARE IN ACCORDANCE WITH

DATE | SIG

OFFICIAL RELATION T ... AAA Gun Bn in which ... Ldr.

D1222273

17. This report has 0 inclosures *(Insert 0 if appropriate)*

18. ENTERED ON WD AGO FORM 66 | D.

DA AGO FORM 67-2, 1 SEP 50

REPLACES DA AGO FORM 67-1, 1 JUL 47, WHICH BECOMES OBSOLETE EFFECTIVE 15 SEP 50.

19885—FEC P&PC—11/51—150M

To Jeanne

These are my precious memories of Joe and my life together for so many wonderful years. I hope you will enjoy it.

Anne Butler Muckerman

A SOLDIER'S SOLDIER
Joseph Edward Muckerman, II

Anne Butler Muckerman

with Anne Hanzel

Acacia Publishing

Library of Congress Control Number: 2012920123

ISBN is 978-1-935089-58-2

Published by Acacia Publishing, Inc.

Gilbert, Arizona

www.acaciapublishing.com

Printed and bound

in the United States of America

Profits from this book will be donated to the Long Gray Line Fund at West Point.

CONTENTS

ACKNOWLEDGMENTS

Without the help of Joe's many friends who shared their memories, this book would not exist. They are mentioned throughout, but special thanks to Tim Cronin (USMA 1949), who supplied so many wonderful stories about his and Joe's West Point years. Tim's memory is as excellent as his sense of humor, and his patience with our many questions exceeds both. Thank you to John McBride for friendship and counsel during difficult days and encouragement to keep moving forward. Uncle Wally Schmieder reached farther back in Joe's history than any of us, remembering Joe as a baby. Thank you to Ted Becker and to David Garner for contributions included in the Tribute section, along with those from our four wonderful Muckerman children, Martha, Ed, Peter, and Lucy, who also contributed to the content in meaningful ways, and grandchildren Emily, Jocelyn, Christian, Caroline, Landon and Hollis, six of the eleven inspirations for this book. Our friends in Lewes, Larry Wiley (USMA 1949) who helped with technical review and Bill Sharkey for guiding us through a broad understanding of the Pentagon and the Department of Defense in the 1990s. John Brinkerhoff (USMA 1950) added essential details about Joe's contribution to mobilization preparedness. Thank you, Bede Toberman, sister, proofreader, and enthusiastic supporter. Gratitude to Sallie B. Jones, benevolent grammarian and supportive friend, and Stephen Hanzel ,who always kept the paper tray full and the ink flowing.

FOREWORD

Joseph E. Muckerman, II

who honored his God, defended his Nation, and cherished his family.

This was a man neither famous nor rich nor powerful, but a man much deserving the biography that his wife of fifty-six years has composed and that you will soon read. Take your time, it covers more than a half century and anecdotes the main themes that are worthy of reflections and remembrance.

Fort Riley, Kansas, home of the 7th Cavalry, was where Joe Muckerman and I initiated our friendship; one lasting sixty-one years until 2010 when he went home to God. We were new second lieutenants when we first met, he from the United States Military Academy at West Point and I from Gonzaga University in Spokane, Washington.

His quiet but distinguished career you will read about in some detail in the following pages. Even a fulsome listing of his assignments and responsibilities is only a skeleton. In no way could it convey his fierce integrity and professional ambition to serve this nation, fully living up to the proud tradition of its armed forces.

Fine model, best of friend, sometimes tutor, Joe made me better for having long association with him. I feel certain that this praise only echoes what many dozens of others would say if asked about this grand man.

It was a privilege to know him, it is a privilege to be called on to pen this introduction. I believe the reader will also be privileged to know Joe vicariously through the reading of this biography.

John P. McBride, SJ[1]

PREFACE

My husband, Joe Muckerman, would be the first to say that he lived a wonderful life. When he learned that his life was almost over, the only regret that he expressed was that he had not carried through with his intention to record a family history for our grandchildren or to write down a few good stories of his own. His hope was to leave something behind for them to know a little more about the man he was, beyond the Grandpa he hoped they would always remember. Joe began to write an autobiography, but his interest in events in the present continually interrupted his recording of those from the past. When our friend Anne Hanzel volunteered to be his writing assistant, he recommitted to his project. Sadly, Joe's illness progressed more rapidly than we had anticipated and this was not to be.

To honor Joe and his wish to "pass on some history to those I love," this is the story of his life. Regrettably Joe's own account of events, from his assignments in post-war Japan through his Pentagon days, is mostly absent. Therefore, our telling of his story remains limited to what we can document from the written childhood memories he left us, U. S. Army documents, including the Official Government File or Performance Data, beginning with his conditional cadet appointment to the United States Military Academy at West Point through his retirement from the Army in 1979, news clippings, letters, photographs, professional resumés, commendations, recollections provided by friends and many co-workers, and of course, my own memories. While this provides a general description of where he was during his career, we have chosen not to draw conclusions about his motivations or opinions unless we could do so with certainty.

The other challenge is to tell this story without glorifying Joe, because that would have embarrassed him deeply. Joe's accomplishments rarely fell out of balance with his humility. People who worked with him will attest to the fact that he did his job —whatever it was at the time—to the best of his ability, always. Success came with some luck and a lot of hard work. It also meant keeping in perspective that work would not replace family and official accolades were ephemeral; love is ever lasting.

Without the help of the many people who loved and admired him, this could not have been written.

Anne Butler Muckerman

INTRODUCTION

Although he never considered himself to be extraordinary, Joe will never be forgotten by those of us who knew him.

Joe Muckerman captured the image of the quintessential American man of his time. Handsome from childhood, he was tall and blue-eyed and possessed a keen intelligence that was balanced with a quiet demeanor. There would be occasions through the years when those blue eyes flashed, but mostly they twinkled.

When recalling him, people often use the word "gentleman." Joe had impeccable manners and a calm voice with a disarmingly slow speech pattern that worked equally well with small children, subordinates, and hot heads. It was not in Joe's nature to act rashly, although in the course of his career he repeatedly proved that he was capable of quick response while under extreme pressure. His humility was genuine but should not be taken for lack of confidence. He had a firm family foundation, a deep faith in God, and a lifetime of military training that did not encourage second guessing.

If there is any mystery about Joe Muckerman, it is what combination of personal qualities and outside influences kept him true to the beliefs that he always had, yet flexible enough not to be buried in what could have been his own rhetoric. In his company one could expect to be engaged in lively conversation on a wide variety of topics. He had an innate talent for drawing out a person and respectfully listening to that person's opinions and perspective. We suspect that this not only served to enlarge his own world view, but also to test it. Often a teacher, he was always a student.

Joe was born in St. Louis, Missouri on July 4, 1926. Growing up, he absorbed the moral and religious values of his parents and of the Roman Catholic Church and the work ethic of the ambitious German-American immigrants who were his ancestors. As an adolescent during World War ll, he was steeped in patriotism. In addition to very loving parents, Joe and his sister Mary Ann basked in the doting attention of their grandmother whose lessons were not only to be good, but to do good.

While Joe's path to the U.S. Military Academy at West Point was not predestined, it seemed an inevitable step into his adulthood. He was not a perfect cadet, but a determined young man who merged his own ethics and morals with the highest standards of military leadership and training. While embodying the ideals of the United States Army, he was not defined by them. Throughout his life he maintained the ability to analyze information and come to his own conclusions, believing that ultimately he served a higher power. Graduating from the Academy in 1949, Joe served for 30 years in the Army. In his second career he joined the faculty of the National Defense University until receiving a Presidential appointment to the Senior Executive Service of the United States Department of Defense. Throughout 45 years of military and government service he received consistent respect and admiration from both superiors and subordinates for his dedication to our country and for his compassionate and instructive leadership.

In 1953 Lieutenant Muckerman married his sweetheart, Anne Butler. Theirs was a marriage of deep love and mutual respect. They built a life and raised a family, moving 10 times during the first 18 years of their marriage before settling in Alexandria, Virginia, and finally moving to Lewes, Delaware. The houses changed frequently but Joe and Anne constructed a solid family foundation for their four children and eleven grandchildren. This is Joe's story, Anne's story, and the story of the life that they made together.

Anne M. Hanzel

Chapter One

An American Boyhood

Sharing a birthday with the Nation he so loved, Joseph Edward Muckerman, II was born on Independence Day, Sunday, July 4th, 1926, in St. Louis, Missouri. He arrived during the period of prosperity and effervescence known as "the roaring 20s." Movies were silent, the country was "dry," and the nation's economy was finally enjoying a strong and optimistic recovery after the First World War. The sun was shining when young Edward Muckerman and his wife Josephine carried home their healthy, first-born child.[1]

St. Louis in the 1920s was comprised of a significant and interconnected German-American population. Joe was third generation American on the Muckerman side and second generation on his maternal Schmieder side. Close family ties and a strong Germanic influence surrounded Joe throughout his childhood. Joe's paternal grandparents maintained a close affiliation with their neighborhood and with the Catholic Church that had been built with funds raised by a community predominately populated by German immigrants or their first generation offspring. Joe's cousin Chris J. Muckerman records that the German language was spoken exclusively in their grandfather Christopher Muckerman's (Joe's great grandfather) home in St. Louis until about 1900.[2]

Joe was only three years old at the time of the stock market crash, the trigger event that is most often identified as the beginning of the catastrophic tumble of the nation's economy into years of hardship.[3] In Joe's recorded memories of his own childhood, his only mention of the Great Depression involved his beloved "Gram," maternal grandmother Anne Springmeyer Schmieder. "After losing much of her inheritance...(Gram) moved into our home." It is possible that the young Muckerman family remained somewhat insulated from the effects of the Great Depression. Joe's father, Edward C. Muckerman, was employed in his family's business, The Polar Ice Company and its sister company, City Ice and Fuel, which distributed essential commodities to city dwellers. Subsequent economic recovery in America was tied to the creation of manufacturing jobs that supplied armaments to Europe in the late 1930s and early 1940s, and St. Louis was ahead of many other cities in recognizing this opportunity.[4] Later Edward Muckerman joined the Manchester Bank as a vice president, landing him in the center of the busy and growing industrial rebirth of the city.

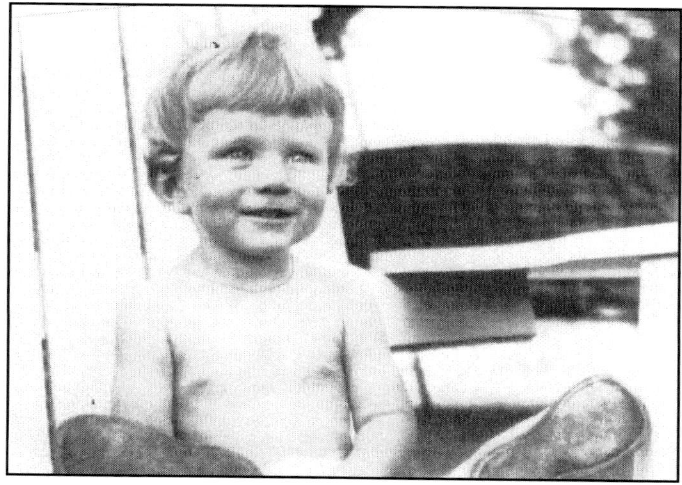

Joe at two.

Joe's earliest memories are of the perennially happy household shared with his parents, "E.C." and "Jo," "Gram," and his younger sister Mary Ann who was born January 28, 1929. In the mid-1930s the family moved to 44 Crestwood Drive in Clayton, Missouri, a pretty suburb located due west of the city limits of St. Louis.[5] In Joe's own written account and by the memories of his sister Mary Ann and Uncle Wally Schmieder (Josephine's youngest brother), it was a very harmonious home. "Gram" was in charge of the kitchen and was second in command of the rest of her daughter's household.

Joe and Mary Ann.

"Dad adored her," Joe wrote, "as did Mary Ann and I. I don't think Dad and Mom spoiled us," Joe recalled, "we always cleaned our plates, did our homework, cut the grass, polished our shoes and made our beds."

At the close of the school year, "Gram," Mary Ann, and Joe traveled by train to the family cottage in Douglas, Michigan. Their job was to clean up the cottage and the grounds in anticipation of their parents' arrival in July when they reunited for the birthday that was also the nation's grandest summer celebration. Uncle Wally remembers going to the fireworks displays with his sister and brother-in-law and a very young Joe. "His father told Joe that the fireworks were for him and that everyone was celebrating his birthday. He believed it for many years."[6]

Anne Springmeyer Schmieder, "Gram."

"Gram," who had been widowed at age 42 in 1919 and finished raising her own three children without their father, undoubtedly provided both stability and considerable experience to her only daughter's household. Joe remembered that "she never bawled us out when we were bad, but explained why we were wrong and gave us jobs around the house to keep us out of mischief. During the summer we took the streetcar to the cemetery where her husband (our grandfather) was buried. We cut the grass around his horizontal tombstone and then we had a picnic lunch."

Gram's husband, Grandfather Schmieder (Franz Josef Schmieder, Jr.), was born in the Austrian Alps in 1871. His own father, Franz Josef, Sr., mother, and three siblings emigrated from Germany in about 1883 after resisting excessive taxation. A miller in his native country, Schmieder, Sr., moved his family to St. Louis where he had contacts in the bakery business. Franz Josef, Jr., became an apprentice baker and married the American-born Anne Springmeyer ("Gram"). Working together, they built a successful wholesale/ retail bakery business. When his health declined, he sold the business to provide stability for his wife and young family.[7]

Joe's father, Edward, "E.C." Muckerman, never knew his own mother, Paula Ruge Muckerman, who died in childbirth. He was sent to live with relatives (the Sanders family). "They took good care of him but he lacked the love only real parents can give. Because of this experience, Dad went out of his way to give Mary Ann and me a lot of attention and love."

Joe as a boy.

Joe attended grade school at Our Lady of Lourdes Parish, walking to school each morning with his best friend Buddy Erker. During his second-grade year, severe ear infections, and missed school days resulted in Joe having to repeat the grade. This unfolded in a humiliating way that he would remember and record 75 years later. "I'll never forget the day that all my friends advanced to third grade and I was told to stay in my seat. I was deeply hurt and humiliated. But in an important way that experience paid off. I said to myself, 'I won't fail again.'"

Mary Ann in 1939.

In all other ways Joe experienced a typical American boyhood, enjoying neighborhood friendships, playing softball and touch football, and occasionally executing harmless pranks. An existing piece of Muckerman memorabilia is a small "newspaper" called The Crestwood Drive News, produced by Editor Joe Muckerman and selling for three cents a copy. Along with various neighborhood comings and goings, Joe wrote a short column reporting that Hitler's army recently occupied Holland. (The Newsletter is undated, but the German army invaded Holland in 1940.)

An extended family of Schmieders and Muckermans lived in the area, including Edward's only full sibling, his sister Clara. Sometime after the death of Edward and Clara's mother, their father, Joseph E. Muckerman, married Anabel Williams. This marriage produced three children: Mary, Joseph J., and John Frederick. When Joseph E. died (around 1939), his will appointed his widow Anabel and his eldest son Edward as co-executors of the estate. This resulted in considerable unhappiness and friction. While the details are lost, the stepmother and siblings had different financial needs and the primary asset in the estate was the deceased's ownership in the family business, now named Polar Wave Ice and Fuel Company. Joe wrote, "On many occasions I asked, 'What's wrong, Dad?' and received the answer, 'The estate distribution. I kicked the covers all night.'"

Joe and Mary Ann in Douglas, Michigan in the 1940s.

Perhaps connected to this but also without detailed explanation, E.C. split from his Muckerman cousins and siblings in management of Polar Wave. When he left, it was to join the Manchester Bank as vice president. This, like the settlement of the estate with his siblings, could not have been an amicable parting, but in Joe's analysis, "Dad got a lot of misery from his relatives but he rose above it and was a great father and husband."

Joe attended high school at St. Louis University High School, an academically rigorous school established and run by the Jesuits. The school was located a short distance from the family home in Clayton.

In 1940 E.C. and Jo built a larger house on a 22-acre parcel in a community named Country Life Acres. This moved them farther northwest of St. Louis, but still within commuting distance. On his return home from the bank each afternoon, E.C. picked Joe up at school. This transportation arrangement prohibited Joe from participating in sports or after-school activities, but Joe worked in the yard and hunted on winter weekends with his friend Tom Aster and his Irish Setter, Mike. That hunting instinct would later get Mike in trouble with one of their neighbors, Branch Rickey, owner of the Cardinals baseball team.

"One day Branch knocked on our door and said that he was going to shoot Mike because Mike had killed 4 of his ducks and then laid them on the Muckerman doorstep. I said, 'Mr. Rickey, you can shoot me but not Mike.'" Whether Branch Rickey's reaction was exasperation or admiration for the young Joe Muckerman, that was the end of the incident.

A teenager growing up in St. Louis during World War II, Joe was extremely influenced by the patriotism of the country and the news reports concerning American soldiers in Europe and in the Pacific. Additionally, wartime defense production had taken over employment in St. Louis with at least 420 St. Louis area plants working on direct defense contracts and as many as 2000 more acting as subcontractors.[8] As Americans fought in Europe and then the South Pacific, the war was not simply a topic of conversation but an element of life as young men "shipped out" and young women joined assembly lines in their absence. In St. Louis wartime production provided a steady paycheck for many family homes.

Joe's uncle Wally Schmieder.

According to Joe's uncle Wally Schmieder, young Joe looked forward to joining the Army as soon as he graduated from high school.[9] It can only be surmised that when he realized the depth of his son's conviction, E.C. did his utmost to make the best of this and come up with an alternate plan for his son.

The possibility of an appointment for Joe to the United States Military Academy at West Point came through Oliver Parks, an aviation pioneer who was a managing partner of Curtis-Steinberg Airport, the first major airport in St. Louis, now the St. Louis Downtown Airport.[10] Parks was also deeply connected to the Jesuit community in St. Louis and a major fundraiser for the establishment of St. Louis University.[11] Whether E.C. and Parks were friends or if they were brought together by a third party, it was through Parks that young Joe's course to West Point was charted.

Joe in Colorado in the summer of 1944.

Dated October 29, 1943, a letter from the Adjutant General's Office of the War Department acknowledges and accepts Joe's "conditional cadet appointment" and advises that he will need to prepare mentally and physically for the requirements of admission.

Joe finished high school in St. Louis in 1944 and a letter dated June 30, 1944, from the War Department to Honorable Calvin D. Johnson, House of Representatives (State of Illinois), acknowledges the nomination of Joseph E. Muckerman as first alternate candidate for the United States Military Academy for admission on July 2, 1945 and advises that he expect to receive instructions for the March 1945 entrance examination.[12]

It is probable that the curriculum at St. Louis University High School was lacking strength in academic areas that would be essential for Joe to enter the United States Military Academy, because in the fall of 1944, Joe enrolled in the Millard Preparatory School in Washington, D.C. Millard was a preparatory school for male students who were honing their skills to pass the entrance requirements for the United States Military Academy. Homer Millard, who was a West Point graduate himself, opened the academy in 1925 for the academic, physical, and spiritual preparation necessary for cadets to succeed at West Point. Millard graduates enjoyed a very high success rate for admission to the Academy.[13] The only surviving document of Joe's time at Millard is a class photograph. There are no records of his performance or letters from Joe while he was enrolled. In two letters written the following year to his mother, Joe suggests that adjustment to Millard was difficult for him and that he had been very homesick.[14]

No records exist of the entrance exams in the spring of 1945, but on Joe's 18th birthday he and his parents signed an affidavit of birth and acknowledgement of his conditional appointment from the 22nd Congressional District of Illinois. The year at Millard had prepared him academically, and perhaps more importantly, prepared him for the long separation from his St. Louis home and the family who cherished him.

Chapter Two

Duty, Honor, Country

In late June, 1945, Joe and his father traveled east, spending two days together in New York City before boarding a train that was crowded with other new cadets bound for West Point. Joe would soon begin his first year in the United States Military Academy. After leaving Joe, E.C. returned to the Hotel Pierre in New York City and penned a letter to his only son. It begins,

> *Dear Joe:*
>
> *It's a little after ten and I just returned from an eventful day at the Point. Certainly it is one I shall always remember for I witnessed the culmination of much effort and many anxious days on the part of both of us.*
>
> *Until you have a son someday who I hope you can be as proud of as I was of you as you entered West Point, you will never know exactly how I felt.*

The long letter shares all the information the anxious and excited father learned during his day as a parent/observer. Eager to keep Joe connected to the Church, "E.C." reports that he sought out and made a connection with Msgr. Murdock and urges his son to follow up. The letter ends with a paragraph that offers some insight into "E.C.'s" motivation for encouraging Joe to attend the Academy.

> *Our two days in New York were wonderful. I shall always remember them as among the happiest I spent. I surely hated to have to leave you there, but better there than waving to you on a boat bound for the Far East.*[1]

Joe's Dad, E.C. Muckerman, in 1949.

Throughout his first full year at West Point, Joe wrote faithfully to his family, recording daily events at the Academy but also replying to their inquiries or to news that had probably been sent in a previous letter. Here, too, the respect and love for his family are always evident. Four years later, when Joe was in Japan, Josephine Muckerman asked her future daughter-in-law to type the text of Joe's letters and arrange them chronologically in a small notebook. The original letters no longer exist but the typed letters provide vivid descriptions of his first year at West Point and the summer spent on maneuvers from Ft. Bragg, North Carolina, to Ft. Worth, Texas; to Biggs Field in El Paso, Texas; and finally to Norfolk, Virginia and the U. S. Navy transport ship, the U.S.S. New Kent. The summer letters are more descriptive and playful because he had more downtime and no academic competition for his attention. In these letters Joe occasionally acknowledges the difficulties, but never complains about the rigors of the requirements. His only consistent negative narrative was written in 1947 about the summer heat in the swamps of South Carolina and his dislike for being aboard ship at the end of that same summer.

If anything, most of the letters are ebullient. His first letter written from

West Point on July 9, 1945, is factual and somewhat tenuous, but by the second letter on July 16 he writes, "I am well except for sore feet and being oh so tired. The food is wonderful. My two roommates are wonderful. Sunday is wonderful because we get about 4 hours to ourselves."[2] In a letter dated July 29, 1945, Joe writes, "You ought to see our daily parade. It is very impressive and you feel that you are part of the Corps. The new detail is made up of a fine group of men. I do not think that you will find a higher type anywhere. The only plebes who bitterly resent the "uppers" are former officers."[3]

Joe and his mom Jo at West Point.

Tim Cronin, a West Point Company M-2 classmate and lifelong friend of Joe's, recalls that "most of the incoming class in 1945 had already been in military service, many in combat. Col. James Lampros, Joe's Beast Barracks roommate, remembers Joe drawing disproportionate attention from upper classmen eager to improve his military bearing and his thinking."[4] Tim, who was 17 when he entered "The Point," admits that he was "10 days out of high school and ready to lick the world. Joe was one year older and had the benefit of Millard's. He always had the conviction that the world was as genteel and as civilized as he was. We were both quickly disillusioned. I, much later, realized how immature I was. Joe retained his gentility."[5]

Joe's life had been sheltered and soft compared to the experiences of some of his classmates, but he was eager to measure up. What he did not express to his parents were the rigors of "Beast Barracks," an experience designed to weed out the weak or ill-suited before the Academy invested further time educating and training them. Or, as remembered by Cronin, "six weeks of hell." Military training for the new cadets began the first day they arrived.

Joe in his "dress whites" in 1947.

Germany had surrendered to the Allied Forces on May 7, 1945. Joe was with his company at Pine Camp (following the six week "Beast Camp") when he heard the news of Japan's surrender (August 15, 1945). In a letter dated August 20, 1945, he writes, "It is very hard to believe the war is really over—it has been so long since peace. The morning of V.J. Day, which was a holy day, we had Mass in the field—it was very impressive."[6]

The cadets who entered West Point in July 1945 did so without the immediate thought of going to war, but soon the greatly decreased need to graduate a high number of combat ready officers produced other anxieties. Tim Cronin writes, "The end of World War II led to a reduced need for second lieutenants, and the Academy, grading on the curve, chopped away at the Class of 1949. Joe was under continuous pressure to stay ahead of the severing blade."[7] 906 cadets had entered this class; 574 would graduate in June 1949.[8]

Joe, jotting down his own memories, recorded this story about his first year at West Point and connected it to his vivid memory of repeating the 2nd grade at Our Lady of Lourdes Parish.

I repeated my pledge that I would never fail again when I flunked Military Topography and Graphics during my first year at West Point. On the way down to take a day-long "turn out" exam, I said to myself, 'I won't fail again.' Just before the exam began, Col. Walter M. Higgins ("Higgie") said, 'Mr. Muckerman, here is a one way ticket home. Turn outs are like musical chairs, when the music stops some people don't have a chair and I believe that you will be one of them.' I looked him straight in the eye and said, 'Colonel Higgins, the only way that you

> will get me out of here is feet first.' Two days later I was told that I had passed and went on to my second year at West Point. In retrospect, I believe his strong words saved me. Col. Higgins probably concluded that this cadet was no quitter.[9]

The Military Academy calendar and curriculum varied from that of a civilian college. The four year program consisted (then and now) of academic, physical, and military training. The nine month academic year at the Academy gave way to a short break followed by extensive summer travel to army posts all over the country and intensive indoctrinations to military disciplines including infantry, artillery, paratrooper training, time aboard Navy troop transport ships, and flights in every type of airplane in the inventory of the Army Air Corps. If the common academic theme was to keep the pressure on, the common theme of summer maneuvers seemed to center on physical discomfort of the participants. Often mere discomfort gave way to considerable danger. These were not war "games" but situations where young men, who had barely left boyhood, trained on equipment and weaponry most recently used in actual combat.

In a letter written home in July 1947, Joe reports on various maneuvers and visits from El Paso, Texas, to Richmond, Virginia, often in circuitous routes and rarely on aircraft that provided smooth flights. He casually writes that "one plane got in trouble and we got the bell to prepare to jump, but fortunately the difficulty was overcome."[10] In a letter written 63 years later, Tim Cronin remembered the same flight with considerably more detail.

> We took off from Fort Knox to go to Stewart Field, West Point's home base. The weather was bad, thunderstorms and lightning, and Stewart Field closed down. M-2, of course, was the last plane to take off. We were instructed to return to Ft. Knox. Navigation aids then were not what they are now. The pilot reported that he was lost. After a while,

bouncing around in the thunder and lightning, the pilot decided we should jump...we found we had 20 guys and 19 parachutes. We picked the two skinniest guys and strapped them together face-to-face with one parachute and prepared to jump. Standing waiting for the green light to signal us to run out the door, we were lost at night over Kentucky's mountains and forest. I kept saying to myself, "Keep your legs crossed!" since we had learned at paratrooper school about the inadvisability of landing astraddle on a tree branch. Then the pilot said he had a radio bearing on Fort Knox and we should stand down."[11]

The only academic elective at the Academy was language. The curriculum had no other variations. Those who made it to graduation left with the degree of Bachelor of Science, Engineering. The first two academic years concentrated on math and science. Many cadets entering in 1945 had already attended college; some had previously passed courses using the same textbooks being used at West Point. Joe remained at a disadvantage, often hovering precariously near the bottom of his class. Flunking one subject would mean automatic expulsion, regardless of one's talents in other subjects. This extended beyond academics to sports. To fail Boxing was as fatal as to fail Trigonometry. Joe and others depended heavily on the extra tutoring help from others in their company.

Another unusual circumstance of West Point life resulted in friendships that lasted for Joe's entire life. Company assignment (the smaller group he would live with, march with, eat with, and be identified with for the next four years) was designated by height. The motivation for this was to achieve the visual effect of uniformity when the men were assembled for parade. Joe was assigned to Company H-2, later renamed M-2 in a Corps reorganization. All members of M-2 were 6 feet 2½ inches or taller. To create the optical illusion of uniform height, the tallest cadets would form the company in the very front and

Company M-2 at the rear of the parade formation. M-2 also found themselves at the rear of anything else that required a lineup.[12]

Their other distinction was the somewhat asymmetric placement of their barracks. All the other barracks lined up in quadrangle formation. According to Tim Cronin, "This all created a contrary attitude and a special esprit. We were decent to the Plebes, enjoyed a counter-culture; we were different and proud of it. The M-2 tradition went back many years. Joe, Dan McGurk, Dick Bowman, Ed Yellman, John Miller, Jeff Simpson, Jim Lampros and I are West Pointers, but we are also proud alumni of M-2."[13]

M-2 Company. Joe is on the far left. First row: Muckerman, Bowman, Bill Earthman, Simpson, Brown, Miller, Tim Cronin. Second row: Bob Ennis, Boag, Ed Yellman, Ford, Ronald, Whitmarsh. Back Row: Frech, Heckman, Swanke, Barnes, Andrus, Dan McGurk.

The motto of the United States Military Academy is "Duty, Honor, Country," but to this Joe always included "God." He faithfully attended Mass during his four years and was remembered by his friends as having a private but consistent faith.

Asked to recall how Joe dealt with the academic pressure at the Academy, Tim Cronin recalls, "Joe was always, always tolerant and even-keeled. He had more than his share of obstacles and challenges, more than the average cadet, but I can't recall any complaining or griping. He met adversity with equanimity...never bitter, no matter what. Always struggling to do his best and coping with whatever came."[14]

In his third year, the academic curriculum shifted in Joe's favor. The more analytical courses of history, economics and law better suited his talents and interests and he was probably able to relax a bit. Life was not all stress at the Academy. Cadets enjoyed the privilege of a fully paid four years at one of the most recognized and prestigious colleges in the world. Their hands-on experiences in a wide variety of situations exceeded those of most Americans. They worked hard but they were rewarded with privileges and experiences far beyond what civilian colleges could provide. They were well fed, and clothed, and enjoyed a high level of respect and recognition from the civilian population, and they attracted a lot of attention from the girls wherever they went.

Joe and his dad, E.C., at Joe's graduation.

Joe's letters home record once-in-a-lifetime experiences: singing with the West Point Choir at St. Patrick's in New York City, marching down Pennsylvania Avenue in parade formation during Harry Truman's inauguration in Washington, D.C., attending Army/Navy football games in Philadelphia, seeing shows on Broadway during leave, sometimes receiving a special rate gratis of an alumnus. Coming from every state in the Union, West Point cadets had an infinite network of social contacts and invitations. Their small government stipend put a little spending money in their pockets and they were ready for adventure and for romance when their hard work was rewarded with an evening or weekend of leave.

In advance of his graduation, Joe was required to choose the branch or specialty of Army service that he would enter. At that time the choices were Artillery, Armor, Corps of Engineers, Infantry, Signal Corps, and Air Force.[15] Each Army branch had a quota. Cadets with the highest academic ranking selected first. In Army parlance, Joe "branched" Artillery. According to Tim Cronin, Air Force had been Joe's first choice but the quota had been filled before Joe was permitted, by virtue of class rank, to select.[16]

Joseph Edward Muckerman II took the oath of office at West Point on June 3, 1949, graduated from the United States Military Academy on June 7, and received orders to attend the Army General School at Ft. Riley, Kansas, followed by Field Artillery Basic Officers Courses, at Ft. Sill, Oklahoma, and Ft. Bliss, Texas. He then received orders for duty in Korea.

Senior portrait.

Joe (far right) at Tim and Gloria Cronin's wedding, immediately after graduation.

Graduation Exercises

TUESDAY, 7 JUNE 1949

Program

1. INVOCATION
   The Reverend Joseph P. Moore
   Catholic Chaplain

2. INTRODUCTION OF SPEAKERS
   Major General Bryant E. Moore
   Superintendent, U. S. M. A.

3. ADDRESS
   General Lucius DuB. Clay

4. GRADUATION ADDRESS
   The Honorable Gordon Gray
   Acting Secretary of the Army

5. PRESENTATION OF DIPLOMAS
   The Superintendent

6. "ALMA MATER"
   Class of 1949

7. THE NATIONAL ANTHEM
   U. S. M. A. Band

8. BENEDICTION
   The Reverend Frank E. Pulley
   Chaplain, U. S. M. A.

Chapter Three

La Vie en Rose

Growing up in St. Louis, Missouri, in the 1940s, young people from affluent families enjoyed a lively but defined social life that included school and country club dances, teas, athletics, movies and many parties. Most activities were enjoyed in group settings, and the term "date" applied more to having an escort than implying a commitment beyond maintaining an even number of boys and girls at a given social event. Joe attended the all-boys school, St. Louis University High School. Three years his junior, Joe's vivacious sister, Mary Ann, attended the all-girls school, Villa Duchesne.[1] This sibling partnership afforded each of them multiple social contacts and both were popular additions to many guest lists.

When Joe left St. Louis for Millard Preparatory School in 1944, Mary Ann was entering her sophomore year at Villa Duchesne. A close friendship developed between Mary Ann and her classmate Anne Butler. In contrast to the tall, blonde Mary Ann, Anne Butler was a petite, doe-eyed brunette with a warm smile. Mary Ann often visited the Butler home on Upper Ladue Road, and Anne similarly was Mary Ann's guest at the Muckerman home in Country Life Acres. This is where Anne Butler first met Joe Muckerman. After setting West Point as his goal in 1943, Joe was only at home in St. Louis sporadically. At West Point the academic year ended in the late spring, followed by a 4-week break. Cadets then reported back in July for field operations that would require the cadet and his entire company to spend the balance of the summer on maneuvers at forts all over the United States.

Anne's earliest memories of Joe were of him cutting grass at the family home. This isn't surprising since half of the 21 acres the Muckermans owned consisted of landscaped lawn. Free labor to supplement the gardeners was expected of the family's son, especially in a household where a strong work ethic prevailed. It wasn't until the spring of 1947 that Anne recalls looking at Joe and seeing him as more than her friend's older brother. "I particularly remember going to a graduation party at Le Chateau in Clayton and seeing Joe in his dress white summer uniform. He looked so handsome—so much more attractive than any of the boys I knew—I think that I decided that night that he was the one for me. I had always dreamed of marrying a tall, blond man with blue eyes and he fit the bill."

The following fall, Joe was a Second Classman (military equivalent of a Junior) at the Academy with the increased privileges and status afforded an upper classman. Mary Ann and Anne were enrolled in Georgetown Visitation Junior College in Washington, D.C. While this also expanded their social horizons and mobility, a strict code of chaperones and permission rules guided their movements. They may have felt a new sense of freedom, but it was within a far more conservative context than what young women experience today. The nuns at "GVC" were still very cloistered. The only males allowed inside the school were the altar boys. Others never made it past the formal parlor where they were received by the young ladies they called on.

Mary Ann Muckerman, Anne Butler, and Brenda Pape in 1948.

With Joe at West Point, Mary Ann at Georgetown

Visitation, and the Pennsylvania Railroad connecting the two points, there were frequent weekends when Joe and some cadets went to Washington or Mary Ann and her friends journeyed to West Point for dances or (in the parlance of the Academy) "hops." Photographs document the first trip Anne Butler made to West Point with Mary Ann for a "hop" in the winter of 1948. Initially Anne Butler joined the fun as a date for Bob Ennis, a cadet friend of Joe's. It was Brenda Pape who was Joe's date, not Anne. We can only imagine when it was that Joe began to look at Anne as someone other than his sister's friend. Schooled in strategy, Joe may have launched his plan further in advance than Anne imagined.

Anne Butler possessed a sweetness and an enthusiasm that was contagious. As the oldest of four sisters she knew how to instigate fun or organize a party, but she also displayed in her earliest diary entries and writings a seriousness that grounded her. She was not flighty or undependable, and she was quite pretty with her dark brown curls, a quick smile, and very large brown eyes. Anne learned to sail on childhood trips to Lake Michigan, played tennis and golf, and possessed the good manners and social skills similar to those that Joe was taught. She was also a Catholic girl and that was an essential requirement for any girl Joe would consider seriously. There is no doubt that he saw her as a very good match.

Joe and Anne at a party after the Army-Navy game.Thanksgiving 1948.

Letters written during this period by Anne Butler to her friend Odile Stewart increasingly mention "Mary Ann Muckerman's brother Joe," including her surprise that she had received a Valentine's Day card from him in 1948. Although she writes of other dances at other places and with other dates, those young men are never mentioned by name.[2] As the months passed, Joe and Anne's interest in each other continued. By November of 1948 photographs show the girls enjoying Thanksgiving dinner at West Point, but by now Joe's arm firmly encircles Anne Butler's shoulders. Casual date status had progressed to "steady."

In January 1949 Joe's West Point class marched in the Truman inauguration parade in Washington. Thanks to the optimism and financial commitment of a Republican Congress that anticipated the election of their candidate, Thomas E. Dewey, the Truman Inauguration was the most expensive and elaborate to date. It also boasted several history-making firsts. It was the first to be nationally televised, it was the first to be openly integrated, and the presidential seal, the one we know today, was introduced in Washington, for the Truman inaugural. After the oath of office and the president's speech, the parade began at 1 pm and stretched seven miles long. More than 600,000 people packed the city, including many from Truman's home state of Missouri.[3]

In spite of coming from solid Republican families, Joe and Anne didn't let politics interfere with their enjoyment of the day. Anne wrote to Odile, "I'll never forget the parade and everything that the dear nuns at Georgetown so kindly let us out to see—it was more fun than anything—especially because Joe was marching in it and I had dinner with him afterwards at the cutest place in the world called the Iron Gate Inn."[4]

Anne with Joe's first car, a Chevrolet convertible.

On another occasion, snuggled in the back of a taxi cab, Joe sang in French to Anne the song "La Vie En Rose." The very romantic lyrics were written and made famous by the incomparable singer Edith Piaf in 1946. "La Vie En Rose" translates literally as "Life In Rose" or colloquially, a life through rose colored glasses. "Give your heart and soul to me, and life will always be, la vie en rose."

Anne graduated from Georgetown Visitation on June 6, 1949. Her parents had remained in St. Louis to attend her younger sister Bede's high school graduation. This worked to Anne's advantage, allowing her to board a northbound train and rush up to West Point for Joe's graduation and "hop" the following day. Joe's appointment as Second Lieutenant, Regular Army, is dated June 3, 1949. They each returned to St. Louis where Joe enjoyed four weeks of leave before attending the Army General School at Fort Riley, Kansas, followed by Artillery Basic Officer's Courses at Fort Sill, Oklahoma, and Ft. Bliss, Texas.

In the summer of 1950 Joe received orders to report to Okinawa, Japan, for fifteen months. This news was not unexpected but it was not happy for the Muckerman family or for Anne. The so-called Korean Conflict, a civil war that had been simmering since Japan's defeat in 1945, was expected to escalate. With the United States unofficially backing South Korea and the Soviet Union backing communist North Korea, tensions were running very high and U. S. troops were already positioned to help defend South Korea. Troops were sent to Korea in what was referred to as a "police action." President Harry Truman did not request Congress to pass a Declaration of War against Korea.

Joe in Yokohama, Japan.

Anne remembers that Joe said to her, "I hate to ask you to wait for me, but would you?" Certainly he knew the danger he would be exposed to but he was also optimistic about returning to Anne and furthering the romance. Yes, she would wait. Fifteen months didn't seem so long when compared to the separations endured and the sacrifices made by so many other couples during the not-very-distant years of World War II.

Joe left for his 15-month assignment to the 37th Antiaircraft Artillery Battalion (90mm), flying first to San

Francisco, then boarding an Army transport flight that took him over the Aleutians to Japan. Before landing, the young soldiers were instructed to make out wills. After he arrived in Japan, Joe was pulled out of the levy for Korea. No explanation exists for this change, but once he established himself at Yokohama, his Officer Efficiency Reports record that his duties expanded and his superior officers increasingly praised his performance. It is Anne Muckerman's belief that one senior officer in particular lobbied very hard to keep Joe in Yokohama. Whether this was a self-serving move on the part of that officer to retain Joe for his own staff or whether that officer was doing his best to keep the promising younger officer from direct combat is unknown.[5]

Joe on Ketakai firing range in Japan.

Anne does believe that it saved Joe's life because the newly minted second lieutenants were sent to the front lines. Sadly, 29 members of the West Point Class of 1949 would lose their lives in Korea.[6]

Joe's 15-month assignment was incrementally extended for a total of three years in Yokohama. Anne remembers, "I had no idea that it was going to be three long years, but I still would have waited for Joe. I was 'head over heels in love' and felt like the luckiest girl alive except for the constant anticipation that he might be sent to Korea at any time.

Joe made no return trips to the states during these three years, and with the exception of a few very rare telephone calls, his relationship with Anne existed exclusively through their letters. Unfortunately only a few cards remain, but one especially meaningful piece of correspondence does survive. In May of 1951, Joe wrote this letter to Anne's father, Henry Butler:

> Dear Mr. Butler,
>
> I know a letter is not the proper way

to ask for Anne's hand. I only wish circumstances would permit me to do the asking in person. You probably will not mind a little variation though – with three more daughters to give away.

Seriously Mr. Butler I know how fortunate I am to have Anne waiting for me, and I also realize that I am asking a great deal to have her wait such a long time. Knowing this I feel it might be easiest if we became officially engaged – thus this letter.

If I had had any sense I would have asked her long ago. And then I would have been able to get your permission in the normal way.

I have about $4000 saved up and will make $325/month when I marry Anne. If things are settled by that time and I can get out of the army, I will go in business with Dad – if not I will probably get a teaching job at Fort Bliss.

The above is about all I can be sure of (except of how I feel about Anne) with things as they are today – except how fortunate I am to be getting you and Mrs. Butler as relatives.

Sincerely, Joe

Anne and Joe shortly after his return.

The engagement was announced in the newspaper on May 27, 1951. The happiness of the official engagement made the spring pass quickly. Jo Muckerman wanted Anne to have the diamonds from her own father's antique stickpin and accompanied

Anne to Jaccard's in St. Louis to have the stones set into an engagement ring. Joe sent a pearl necklace from Mikimoto in Japan. Anne's parents gave an engagement party with the prospective groom 6,000 miles away.

Anne accompanied Mary Ann (Muckerman) Wrapp and the Muckermans to Estes Park, Colorado, for several weeks in the summer of 1951. This was her first visit there and she wrote to Odile Stewart of her delight in being able to see a place that Joe loved. She wrote letters to Joe every three or four days and received as many back from him. He wrote about the magic of Japan and she wrote about the familiar patterns of home life; they confided their dreams, confessed loneliness for each other, and planned their future letter by letter.

Anne as a debutante.

Waiting month by month for Joe to return from Japan and for married life to begin, Anne sometimes wondered if she would ever be a bride. "Two of my younger sisters, Sissy and Bede, were married now. Being the oldest, I was getting anxious, and friends were always asking when it would be my turn." Girls married at a younger age during these years and one was considered an "old maid" if she hadn't married by age twenty-five, but Anne remained unwavering in her choice. She was not in the position to make any long-term employment commitments, but she needed ways to make the time pass. Along with her friends Kit Bull and Franny Clarkson, she operated a small nursery school out of Martha Butler's converted studio[9] and used her mother's big station wagon to transport their little students. Another short-lived occupation was as a retail clerk behind the blouse counter at Famous-Barr, a St. Louis department store. At that time merchandise was displayed in glass-fronted cabinets, and the customer would ask the sales clerk to supply the proper size. This occupation was also short lived. Anne quit when she received a transfer to the Bakery Department.

The following year, Anne flew to Ft. Sill, Oklahoma, staying with Brad and Marilyn Terry, close friends of Joe's from Japan. In a letter to Joe in Japan from Brad Terry dated February 17, 1953, Brad wrote with great enthusiasm about the visit and how much fun he and Marilyn had with Anne.[8] Eager to fit in, Anne read books about Army life. She read about the protocol of being a perfect Army wife, including the basics of a proper wardrobe that included hats and gloves to wear to official functions and the importance of having calling cards and how to properly present them with the corner turned down in a special way. The thought of fulfilling this grown-up role was intimidating, but also exciting, and she looked forward to embarking on her new life with Joe, far away from St. Louis.

Mrs. Ferguson Butler
requests the honour of your presence
at the marriage of her daughter
Anne Jocelyn
to
Joseph Edward Muckerman, II
Lieutenant, United States Army
on Thursday, the fifteenth of October
one thousand nine hundred and fifty-three
at eleven o'clock
Church of the Annunziata
Saint Louis

As the country grew increasingly restless about Korea and American involvement and cost became political "hot potatoes," Joe still waited monthly to be sent home. Anne recalls that during this time period each day weighed heavily, but looking back now, three years seem like a short prelude to the life that would follow. For all the long months in St. Louis at 18 Upper Ladue, Anne counted the days with letters always to Joe with news of the day and how she looked

Church of the Annunziata.

forward to seeing him again. The letters were Anne's only contact with Joe and they had to be perfect. "My sisters made fun of how I wrote each letter in scratch first and then rewrote them before mailing them," Anne remembers.

Finally, an armistice was signed on July 27, 1953 and Anne felt confident enough about Joe's return to shop for a wedding dress. She found it in a store in Clayton for the extravagant sum of $150. Her happy anticipation during the final weeks of summer was so heightened that the dress would have to be altered weeks later to accommodate her weight loss.

But it was not until September 16th that Anne received a telegram informing her that Joe would be arriving home the following day, September 17, 1953. Finally! If Anne had any serious apprehension about Joe as she waited for his train to pull into Wabash Station, she does not recall it now. Bede Toberman still recalls waiting with Anne as the passengers disembarked. Anne was suddenly nervous because she had been teased that after three years' separation, she and Joe might not recognize one another. As soon as they met each other's eyes, though, Joe and Anne ran to each other and embraced. Anne remembers that even though he looked exactly as she remembered him, she needed to touch him to be sure that he was really there. Wabash Station became the end of his first tour of duty and the beginning of the rest of his life with Anne. She was so overcome to have him home that she didn't even mind what she had previously considered his only truly bad habit—smoking the occasional cigar.

Joe had used none of his leave for three years, but Army restrictions prohibited him from taking more than 60 consecutive days before reporting to Ft. Sill, Oklahoma, so it was time for another type of mobilization. The eldest Butler sister was finally getting her wedding. When Joe arrived in St. Louis it was an occasion for much joy and many parties to celebrate his safe return and the long-awaited marriage. Close friends arranged bridal showers where Anne gratefully received all the kitchen treasures available for the times, many of which she still uses. Details of the wedding that had been dreamed about for two and a half years would be set into motion.

During these years, hats for ladies were essential fashion accessories and a must for church weddings. A few days before the wedding it was discovered that the mother of the bride and the mother of the groom had purchased identical hats to wear to the ceremony. Once this coincidence was discovered, Anne's mother quietly exchanged hers for another.

Jo Muckerman and Martha Ferguson Butler.

The wedding occurred on the morning of Thursday, October 15, 1953, a beautifully crisp but sunny fall day. It was the first wedding at the new Church of the Annunziata in St. Louis. In spite of the short planning time, the wedding was large and the church beautifully decorated. Floor standard vases filled with large white chrysanthemums welcomed guests at the entrance to the chancel of the church. The candlelit altar was flanked by white chrysanthemums and masses of woodwardia ferns were banked in the sanctuary as a setting for the ceremony. Lemon foliage and white satin bows

Married at last
–October 15, 1953.

marked the pews of the center aisle down which the bridal party walked.

Anne wore a long white satin gown and the lace veil that her mother had worn in 1927, and Joe was in uniform. Joe's best man was his brother-in-law, Jack Wrapp. Matron of Honor, Joe's sister Mary Ann Wrapp, and bridesmaids, Anne's sisters Sissy, Bede, and Judy, wore burnt orange lace dresses and carried bouquets of fall flowers. Anne's young cousin Carol Lynn Ferguson dressed in a yellow frock, served as flower girl. Joe's Uncle Wally Schmieder, childhood friend Bud Erker, and brother-in-law Nick von Guggenberg were Joe's groomsmen.

The wedding mass was conducted by Msgr. Charleville B. Faris who was the beloved longtime pastor and friend of the couple. Anne recalls that during the ceremony she felt that she had never been as happy as she felt during those moments and she silently thanked God for answering her prayers and bringing Joe safely back home to her. A luncheon reception and dancing followed at the Glen Echo Country Club. Later that evening Anne's mother, Martha Butler, had a dinner party for the out-of-town guests at her home, #3 Upper Ladue Road. All of the wedding gifts were displayed in the hall. This was standard practice, inviting all of the guests to admire the gifts.

One event did cast a shadow over the wedding planning. Anne's parents had divorced earlier that year and their relationship remained unsettled. In order to spare everyone else's feelings and focus all attention on the newlyweds, Henry Butler did not attend the wedding. Anne walked down the aisle with her uncle, Louis A. Ferguson. After the wedding reception, Anne and Joe visited Henry privately.[10]

Genevieve Janes and Anne's younger sister Beatrice (Bede).

The following day, Anne dressed in the appropriate "going away suit" of the day with a very fashionable marten fur stole that Joe had sent months earlier from Japan. Driving the new Ford coupe that was a wedding gift from both of her parents, Anne and Joe set off for the Broadmoor Hotel in Colorado Springs for a short honeymoon[11] and a love affair that would last for the next 56 years. Starry-eyed and optimistic, Anne left her old life behind and they hit the road for "La Vie en Rose."

Joe's interest in an Army career had deepened during his three years in Japan, but he had reservations about Anne's happiness as an "Army wife." Marriage requires flexibility and strength beyond what most young people ever envision when the vows are spoken and rings exchanged. Every marriage has its unique challenges, but the partner of a career Army Officer must possess qualities that include adaptability to frequent moves, separations, and the possibility that a spouse may suddenly receive orders to report to a combat zone.

Jack Wrapp, Joe, and Mrs. Philip Smith admire wedding gifts.

When they married in 1953, Joe had fulfilled three years of his four-year active duty commitment to the Army. He had promised Anne and her father that if she did not like the Army life they would return to St. Louis and, for Joe, a position with E.C. at the Manchester Bank. Joe needn't have worried about the back-up plan because Anne faced the future with enthusiasm. She had waited three years for her lieutenant, watched two of her sisters marry and leave home, read countless letters from Joe in Japan, and was ready to join him wherever the road led.

Throughout his 45 years of government service, Joe's ability to select qualified staff people and to mentor promising protégés would be repeated at every posting, but no choice would ever prove as important as the one he made when he chose Anne Butler for his wife and partner.

Chapter Four

The Army Life's For Me!

During his years at the Academy Joe fought his share of academic battles to retain his place with the class of 1949, but his determination proved tougher than the obstacles he had to cross. If there were those who questioned his career longevity in the Army, Joe never listened. After graduating in June 1949 he attended the standard courses at the General School at Ft. Riley, Kansas, the Field Artillery Basic Officers Courses at Ft. Sill, Oklahoma, and at Ft. Bliss, Texas, before returning to St. Louis for a short leave in advance of what would become three years in Japan.

Yokohama, Japan

Anne recalls, "I lived the army life vicariously through letters written on many pages of blue air mail stationery. In retrospect, I realize how carefully censored Joe's letters to me would have been, but it was clear that Joe loved being in Japan." The country held infinite fascinations and he was dedicated to the work he was doing. Joe served there during a unique period of time when Japan was undergoing post-World War II reconstruction and at the same time providing the

U.S. military with supply points and defense locations against North Korea. At any given time high-ranking Military or civilians sent from Washington might pass through. During one such motorcade Joe received his first and most historic "dressing down."

As Joe would tell it, the busy domestic life of the citizens of Yokohama streaming daily along the roadways included many pedestrians, bicycles, and more than a few farm animals to slow the path of motor cars and trucks. Often official motorcades were not very indulgent of this pace. For reasons of safety during the course of escorting one convoy through the busy city streets, Joe made the decision to have the drivers exercise their horns and sirens to alert the foot traffic that the motorcade was advancing. In fairly short order, an irate reprimand (never officially entered) that was more commonly known as a "chewing out" came down the line from none other than General Douglas MacArthur. Newly arrived in Japan, Joe was not aware that the General had issued an order that the only motorcade allowed to receive "sirens" was one in which the general himself rode. Luckily for Joe, their paths would never cross again; General MacArthur was relieved of his command in April 1951, returned to the United States, and entered into retirement.[1]

After three years Joe finished his tour as First Lieutenant, Commanding Officer of the 37th AAA Gun Battalion (90 mm). His commanding officer, Colonel H. B. Hudiburg, requested that a letter be attached to Joe's final Efficiency Report to further acknowledge the potential he saw in the younger officer. He wrote, "Rather than discuss individual traits, characteristics, and performances, I can most readily summarize these matters by stating that Lt. Muckerman more closely approaches the theoretical officer, in all aspects, than any other officer I have known. He is the most outstanding officer I have known in his rank and experience level, and he is fully qualified now to assume the duties and responsibilities of a field grade officer."[2]

A few pictures remain of Joe in Japan. The letters we exchanged are gone and Joe's own slides taken during that year were later lost during one of our moves when a packing box was stolen.

Ft. Sill, Oklahoma—Home of the U.S. Army's Field Artillery

Joe reported to Fort Sill on the Monday after we were married. He was assigned as Executive Officer in a 155 mm gun battalion and was soon promoted to Captain. We moved into our first home in "Artillery Village" across from Brad and Marilyn Terry, Joe's best friends from Japan. I had met the Terrys on an earlier visit when Joe was still in Japan and I liked them both a lot. We did everything with them including Thanksgiving dinner and all the holiday celebrations. Brad and Marilyn grew up in regions of Arkansas and Texas and served me my first meal of black-eyed peas and greens. Joe and I were happy in our little house except when the dust storms came up and left enough dust for us to see footprints all across the dark brown concrete floors.

Joe attended Field Artillery Advance Career Course in the summer of 1954. The rating officer wrote that "Captain Muckerman is a superior officer who is held in esteem by officers and enlisted men. This officer has excellent physical stamina. All problems confronting (him) are approached in a logical, methodical manner after careful scrutinizations [sic] and analysis. [He] is very calm and calculating, always achieving outstanding results."[3] At the completion of Artillery and Guided Missile School at Ft. Sill, Joe ranked 6th in his class of 201 participants.[4]

Martha Mary Muckerman, age three, with Shane.

I was working on a pretty important project of my own. Baby Martha Mary Muckerman arrived on the morning of December 24. This was the most joyous and thrilling event of my then 26 years of life. She weighed 8 pounds, 11 ounces, and was a beautiful blonde, curly- haired baby. Joe carried all the gifts right into my hospital bed at the civilian hospital in Lawton. I recall that we received nine boxes of Mavrakos candy from the legendary St. Louis chocolatier. I guess people didn't know what else to send us.

I'd heard frightening stories about the base hospital at Ft. Sill and was not going to risk having my first child there. Like all new parents, we felt Martha was the most special baby ever born. Joe wouldn't let anyone get too close for fear of germs. We learned that all of our babies would be every bit as special and luckily we also learned to relax.

Joe had orders to attend a course at Fort Bliss in Texas from January through March of 1955. My mom came out to Lawton to accompany the baby and me back to St. Louis where we stayed for three months. I missed Joe terribly but we couldn't afford to rent two places.

The Pentagon—Washington, D.C. (Arlington County, Virginia)—Headquarters of the Department of Defense

Joe had previously been nominated to be an aide to President Dwight Eisenhower, but unexpectedly someone else (undoubtedly with more clout) received that highly coveted appointment. In the summer of 1955, Joe was assigned to an interesting job at the Pentagon.

Before being elected President of the United States in 1953, Dwight Eisenhower was a five-star general in the U.S. Army and Supreme Commander of the Allied Forces in Europe, planning and supervising the invasion of France and Germany. In 1951 he became the first Supreme Commander of NATO and in 1952 entered politics. Increasingly alarmed about the growing world presence of the Soviet Union, the United States was engaged in the crusade against communism. These were the early years of the Cold War and Eisenhower was already a national hero—a General with a high credibility factor. He took the 1952 presidential election by a landslide.

National defense remained a critical topic in Washington. The potential for launching missiles into space had grown from scientific advances during World War II. After the war there were considerable secret negotiations at work to remove top scientists from Germany. Naturally both of the biggest world powers, the United States and the Soviet Union, had wanted to secure these scientists for their respective countries, even if it meant obscuring the difficult issues of whether or not the scientists should be considered war criminals.

While the Eisenhower Administration attempted to lead a pioneering and cooperative international scientific organization whose goal was to share information, the Soviets surprised everyone on October 4, 1957, by successfully launching Sputnik 1, the first artificial satellite, into orbit at an elevation of 900 kilometers. This was followed by Sputnik 2 on November 2, 1957.[5]

Joe had been assigned to the Office of the Chief of Staff, Staff Communications Branch at the Pentagon along with Barney Broughton and Jack Waltz and others. Their group was made up of four teams of officers who worked around the clock processing all incoming and outgoing electronically transmitted messages for the entire Defense Department, including staff from the Air Force, Navy and Marine Corps. Joe and Barney were assigned to the same team, the 11:30 pm - 7:30 am shift. Barney never adapted to the schedule and transferred out after a year, although his friendship with Joe lasted a lifetime. "I had great difficulty staying awake, especially at 2 am. Joe was bright and alert all night and helped to keep me from falling asleep. He was always interesting and it was a real pleasure to work with Joe."[6]

One project that Joe was involved with in 1956 was the Annual Civil Defense Training Exercise. Since the fear of attack from the former Soviet Union was so great in those days, civil defense evacuation plans were made for cities and towns all over the United States. In Washington this included the evacuation of 10,000 government employees. The exercises included a tracking simulation of airplanes flying from military bases in the Soviet Union to targets in the United States. In those days the flight time was estimated to be approximately 8 hours. Joe remained on duty in the Army Staff Communications Office where information was channeled to the Joint Chiefs of Staff and to the Advance Headquarters of the three armed services during the six-day exercise.[7]

We were able to rent a townhouse that we loved on South Columbus Street in Alexandria, Virginia. We had wonderful neighbors and happy times. With Joe working all night, he needed to sleep during the day. This necessitated my taking Martha for very long baby carriage rides through Old Town in order for Joe to have some uninterrupted hours of sleep. Martha enjoyed removing her shoes, and when my attention wandered we sometimes returned home without a shoe.

We spent all of our holidays with Aunt Mary and Uncle Alan Ferguson and our cousins, Margay, Sharon, and Carol Lynn at their lovely Chevy Chase home. It was especially wonderful at Christmas when the girls eagerly showed us all their gifts. We felt particularly close to Carol Lynn who had been the flower girl at our wedding. The family dog was a beautiful Irish Setter named Shane, and I love the photo we have of Martha sitting on the stairs with him.

E.C. Muckerman and his namesake, Ed in 1961.

Edward Christopher Muckerman II was born at Alexandria Hospital in Old Town on November 16, 1957. He weighed 10 pounds, 12½ ounces. and was so big that newborn baby clothes wouldn't fit him. Ed was blonde too, with hazel eyes. He was named for Joe's father which made "E.C." very happy. Martha loved her baby brother and was happy to entertain him, which became very useful as his little feet were turned in slightly and the recommended procedure at that time was to put the baby's legs in casts, supposedly to eliminate the need for orthopedic shoes later on. These casts were removed and replaced with new ones every week for six weeks at Walter Reed Medical Center. I was thrilled to have a boy after growing up with three sisters, and Ed, who frequently had an impish look in his eyes, was "all boy" from the start.

In Washington there was considerable pressure for a successful space launch. Trailing behind in the Space Race was demoralizing for Americans. Beyond the issue of pride was the larger concern of falling behind technologically. I knew that Joe and everyone he worked with were under a lot of pressure, but I didn't know any of the specifics. Joe's work was classified and I learned quickly that there would be much about his work life that he could not talk about with me. Much later I read the news stories along with everyone else, but it would be years before Joe talked about this or many other classified events that occurred during his years in the Army.

Testing for the U.S. Project Vanguard booster rocket was not going well. The first two launches ended with explosions. On January 31, 1958, the launch of Explorer I occurred from Cape Canaveral, Florida. Explorer was a very different type of satellite developed by former Nazi Werner von Braun and his team of recently immigrated German scientists. The satellite carried equipment that transmitted signals back to earth for tracking purposes. At the Pentagon, along with von Braun and Secretary of the Army Wilbur M. Brucker, Captain Joe Muckerman was in attendance, monitoring the progress of the launch and the first successful flight of a U.S. spacecraft.

A certificate accompanied a letter from Secretary Wilbur Brucker to Captain Muckerman in 1958 admitting him into the Concatenated Fraternity of Master Missileers, Pentagon Chapter, stating that the recipient had been "duly and properly initiated into the most exclusive fraternity in the world" and proclaiming that he had "now attained the exalted rank of Master Missileer."[8] I had it framed and it hangs in our house now. While tongue-in-cheek in execution, it expresses the excitement and pride of a group of men who had witnessed the beginning of America's entry into space exploration.

Concatenated Fraternity of Master Missileers Circa 1958 Pentagon Chapter

To All To Whom These Presents Shall Be Exhibited: Greetings!

Inasmuch as Captain Joseph E. Muckerman has duly petitioned to be admitted to the rites and ceremonies of our Sublime Concatenated Fraternity, and has been found to possess the intestinal fortitude demanded of a Master Missileer, and

Since he kept vigil before a teletype-writer in the Pentagon for Four Solid Hours from 2130 January 31 until 0130 February 1 in the year 1958; and did at such time and place do all in his power by main strength and awkwardness to lift, boost, elevate and launch the Jupiter-C satellite Explorer into orbit.—

Now, Therefore, from and after this date be it known that he has passed through all the sublime mysteries and has been duly and properly initiated into the most exclusive fraternity in the world, thereby entitling him to all honors which do now or may later accrue by reason of his perspicarity as well as the coincidence of his physical presence during the above probationary period of Four Solid Hours!

Accordingly, let it be proclaimed that he now has attained the exalted rank of Master Missileer and shall henceforth enjoy an AA-1 seating priority at all future Pentagon satellite launchings, with the privilege of double oxygen rations on the first United States Army ship to penetrate the celestial frontier enroute to the moon. Also, he is entitled to repeat ad infinitum to all and sundry persons every detail of all of the events leading up to, during, and following the launching of said Jupiter-C satellite Explorer. — {and to make any desirable elaboration thereon to suit his fancy, provided he adheres somewhat closely to the agreed facts}.

Done at the City of Washington, D. C. this 28th day of March AD 1958

By Jupiter!

Wilber M. Brucker.

Wilber M. Brucker
Chief Master Missileer
Concatenated Fraternity of Master Missileers
Circa 1958, Pentagon Chapter

A few months later we went to a gala party where the first prize was a trip for two to Miami, Lima, or Nassau. The time was getting close to midnight and Joe wanted to go home, but I convinced him to stay a little longer. When they called the number on my ticket I was so surprised that I could hardly walk up to claim the prize. My legs were like rubber.

Peter was only six weeks old at the time of that trip. I had made friends with a woman who was a teacher in Panama who came to stay with the children, and Bienvenida was there as well. The week in Lima, Peru, was truly marvelous. We took a side trip to Juan Cayo, travelling up to 15,000 feet in altitude, riding in a train with open windows and certainly no additional oxygen. We just sat there virtually immobile. The native men had huge chests that we guessed were needed to accommodate their expansive lungs. The open air markets were so colorful.

On the train back to Lima a man pushed against Joe as he was lifting our bag overhead. After the man rushed by, Joe felt for his wallet but it was gone. We had nothing at that point. A fellow passenger very kindly allowed us to cash a check to him so that we would have some money. He worked for the Grace Company, and we will never forget his kindness. It took another six weeks before we received a refund for the stolen traveler's checks.

Martha and Ed watch a ship traverse a lock at the Panama Canal.

A day or two later was St. Rose of Lima Day, quite a big holiday. Cardinal Cushing was there to say Mass. Standing in the crowd, Joe could feel hands trying to pick his pocket but this time there was no wallet to find. We did manage to purchase some beautiful Mexican silver there.

In Panama we often went into Balboa on a Saturday to have lunch at the beautiful old Hotel Tivoli and browse the shops. One merchant had a black console bar inset with stones that Joe loved. Since Joe had a pair of madras plaid pants that the merchant was coveting, they made a swap on the spot. Every Sunday morning Joe took the children to see the ships go through the canal or to the beach. They all loved their special time with him and he adored them.

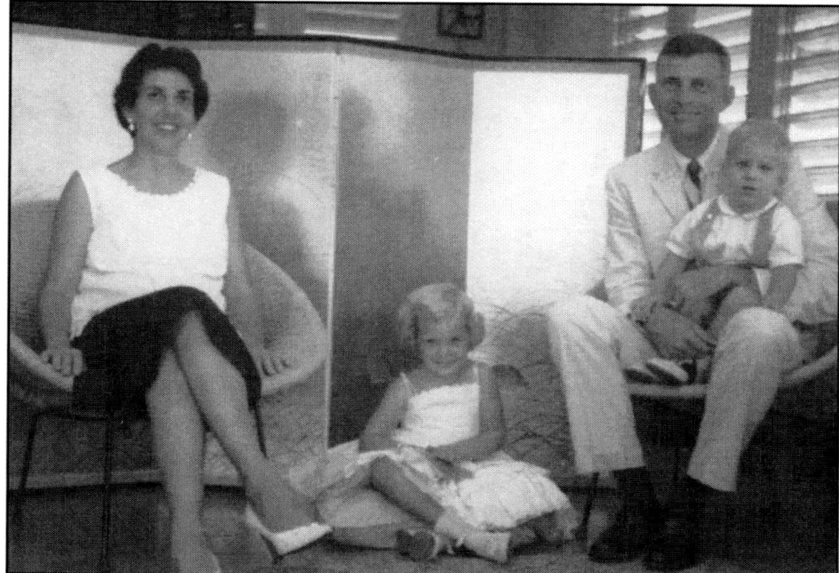

Anne, Martha, Joe, and Ed at home in Panama.

Another purchase made possible after Joe received some inheritance money from his paternal grandmother was a gorgeous silver tea service found at Mercurio's in Balboa. This set had also been made in Mexico and was very heavy. Like everyone else stationed in the Canal Zone during those years, we also acquired a big hammered brass table, a carved teak screen, and an aluminum Christmas tree.

Performance Data reports from that time indicate that Joe had secured the attention of higher ranking officers for performance of duties and for his leadership skills. "I would rate this officer in the upper 1/12th of the captains in the Artillery."[9] "His steadiness, dependability and unending devotion to duty have gained the respect of juniors and seniors alike." Also, recorded without subtlety, was our Muckerman partnership: "Captain and Mrs. Muckerman recognize their social responsibilities and set an excellent example for other officers and their wives."[10]

Joe's personal style of leadership was already set. Although he would be loath to concede that he was anyone special, he would have been honored to read how he was remembered over 50 years later by Joe Cunningham who had been a young lieutenant serving under Joe in Panama. "Joseph E. Muckerman ll has been my hero from those three years in Panama. A true gentleman, a deep thinker with the ability to deal with senior officers, young military officers, enlisted personnel, plus political and diplomatic personnel. He has been a role model whom I have tried to emulate." [11]

Joe received his promotion to Major in June 1961 and we left Panama with many wonderful memories and one more baby than when we had arrived. In August Joe received his first Army Commendation Medal for Meritorious Service at Ft. Clayton for the period October 1, 1958 to June 13, 1961. Joe's next assignment was to the school at Ft. Leavenworth in Kansas.

Ft. Leavenworth, Kansas—United States Army Command and General Staff College

"Since its inception in 1881 as the School of Application for Infantry and Cavalry, the Command and General Staff College has evolved to meet the educational and operational needs of the United States Army. Since World War II, it has generally been known as the school for Army majors, though the college contains other schools and it educates officers from other military services and from other countries." [12]

During our first year at Ft. Leavenworth we lived on Esplanade Street overlooking the broad Missouri River. The school year was fun with many activities for staff and students. We got to know our neighbors in town, Jean and Ormand Leavel and Jean's daughter, Kathy English. Jean was previously married to a classmate of Joe's, Alan English. In Kansas we experienced many tornado alerts that drove us into the basement. These were the years of bomb shelter panic following the Cuban Missile Crisis that occurred in October of 1962, and emergency drills would also frequently send us underground.

We would stay at Leavenworth for two more years with Joe joining the faculty. We moved on post to a lovely big apartment. Joe worked very hard during this period. The arms race with the Soviet Union and aftermath of the Cuban Missile Crisis kept the country poised for the possibility of combat. Joe received his second Army Commendation Medal and Citation for outstanding and meritorious performance of duty while serving the U.S. Army Combat Developments Command Combined Arms Group from July 14, 1962, to July 31, 1964.

Joe continued to impress superior officers, and his performance reviews during this period reflect his outstanding ability to methodically analyze a problem and organize solutions to many complex and diverse components while maintaining his usual composure. "It should be especially recognized that although he is relatively junior in rank, he has demonstrated unusual ability in dealing with complex studies that are vital." "He should be promoted ahead of his contemporaries."[13] It was recommended that he attend the Armed Forces Staff College.

Wherever we lived we were always active in the community. The kids joined in sports and we were always welcomed into the church. While we were at Ft. Leavenworth Joe acted as sponsor for Lt. Col. Jose Ferero, who was in the Colombian Army.

That summer Peter got the mumps. Strangely enough, my sister Sissy who was living in New Jersey and all of her seven children also came down with mumps at the same time. None of us had them when we were children so the "handwriting was on the wall." Martha swore she would not get them but within three weeks she did, followed by Joe and Ed. The day friends were to arrive, I awoke with a sore jaw and before long all of us had mumps and felt terrible. My good friend Pam Reese lived up the street. "Let me take Peter," she offered, and he went to stay at her house until the rest of us recuperated. Peter was due to have his tonsils removed because he was often sick, but new orders for Joe resulted in our move from Kansas in July 1964 and Peter still has his tonsils.

Vietnam—The United States Military Assistance Command, Saigon, Pacific Command

"The Vietnam problem" was a hot potato item inherited by President Lyndon Johnson when John F. Kennedy was assassinated in November 1963, but the complicated relationship between Vietnam and the United States began far earlier. Financial and other support to South Vietnam had

escalated through the late 1950s and early 1960s based on the belief in the "Domino Theory"—if all of Vietnam fell to control of the communist North Vietnamese, the surrounding countries of Laos, Cambodia, and Thailand would quickly follow. As it became a large issue of debate throughout the 1964 presidential campaign between Barry Goldwater and Lyndon Johnson, more Americans became aware of the existence of Vietnam, even if they did not understand the American political and military debate for being there. It is generally believed that President Johnson strategically decided not to further escalate American military presence in Vietnam during an election year. This was the political climate in the United States in 1964 when Joe was assigned to be a Sector Advisor to the Vinh Binh Sector of the Republic of Vietnam, advising both the Province Chief and the Vietnamese Sector Commander.

It might be assumed that as a military wife I had a greater awareness of what was going on in Vietnam. In fact, this is not correct. First, there was much information that Joe had that was classified and that he did not reveal. Second, Joe did not want me unduly alarmed. His instinct was always to protect us, so he downplayed the dangers of these orders. Nonetheless, I was aware that this was no ordinary assignment and that this was the greatest danger Joe would be exposed to since he boarded the plane in 1949 that we thought would take him to Korea.

When Joe received orders for Vietnam we decided to move to Virginia where I could be close to my mother who was living in Georgetown at the time. We moved into a darling Tudor house at 36 Woodmont Road in a subdivision of Alexandria called Belle Haven. I loved it there. The neighbors were lovely and I felt that the children were safe. However, the day that Joe left for the Far East in October of 1964 was one of the saddest days ever.

The time spent with my mother was very happy and keeping up with three little children kept my worries about Joe from surfacing too often. During that year the City of Alexandria changed the street numbers and our address became 6111 Woodmont Road. I was always so afraid that Joe's letters wouldn't get to me. They were my lifeline to him. Mom and I did everything together, including a month spent at Rehoboth Beach,

Delaware. The kids enjoyed a carefree month going to art school, walking the boardwalk, and going to the boardwalk arcade, Funland. This was in sharp contrast to what Joe was doing a world away.

Vinh Binh Province in the Mekong Delta had a population of 541,000 people and a geographical area of roughly 1700 square miles. The area was divided into six sectors or provinces in what the Army called the 41st Divisional Tactical Area. (By 1976 Vinh Binh and Vinh Long Provinces had been combined and renamed Cuu Long. Currently it is a rice growing area.) Joe's senior officer wrote of him, "Each had a senior advisor and of all of the six, Lt. Colonel Muckerman was by far the most proficient."[14] Joe's sector had the heaviest concentration of Viet Cong, making it the most dangerous. He was able to establish excellent relations with his Vietnamese counterpart, the Province Chief. He accompanied troops into the field on operations against the Viet Cong on numerous occasions and "established a solid reputation among the Vietnamese and the American advisors as a calm professional in a combat situation."[15]

The Proficiency Reports written during Joe's year in Vietnam provide a good description of his duties and the success with which he coordinated and organized his command and worked with people from different U.S. agencies and the South Vietnamese. Given the success of his assignment and the high regard with which he was held, I feel grateful that his tour was only for one year. In August of 1965 he was promoted from Major to Lt. Colonel, and at the end of his tour he learned that he was to be awarded the Vietnamese Cross of Gallantry for services to the 9th Vietnamese Division, and the U.S. Army's Legion of Merit medal for exceptionally meritorious conduct in the performance of outstanding services.

Joe returned safe and sound in September 1965. I met him in San Francisco for some "R & R," followed by a stop in Colorado to see his parents before we returned home together. Unbeknownst to me, the babysitter who had been well recommended and was now "in charge" of the children was an alcoholic who spent most of her time collapsed on the couch.

Our ten-year-old daughter Martha was managing to prepare the meals, and Mom was worried but didn't want to ruin our trip by telling us. The woman drank everything in sight, including the vanilla extract! After we arrived home and I questioned her about it, I decided not to pay her the full amount. Later I saw that she had cashed my check at the liquor store.

Key West, Florida—Army Air Defense Command (ARADCOM)

In the fall of 1962 when United States intelligence discovered a massive buildup of Soviet missiles on the island of Cuba, it was also realized that the southernmost shores of the United States were woefully vulnerable to attack. An immediate response to the Cuban Missile Crisis (October 15 – 29, 1962) was the relocation of HAWK missiles to Key West from Homestead, Florida. Initially a hastily improvised collection of Army weaponry, dilapidated buildings, and canvas tents, by 1965 permanent facilities had been constructed, but the four batteries of the 6th HAWK Missile Battalion were still struggling for organization.

Joe was assigned to Key West, Florida, in November 1965. He had command of the Hawk Battalion and was the top ranking Army officer there. During the Change of Command Ceremony on the field at Boca Chica, Joe was presented with the Legion of Merit medal and the Vietnamese Cross of Gallantry for his service in Vietnam. After our year of separation, being together was award enough for me, but Key West was really a dream assignment. We enjoyed many perks due to Joe's rank and we loved everything about our Key West neighbors and the island lifestyle. Our quarters were right on the water on the coral beach. We had a dock and we purchased a Sunfish sailboat that was really fun. When we occasionally experienced island fever we could take a short flight to Miami.

Performance Reports show that Lt. Colonel Muckerman assumed command of the battalion after a period of "personnel turbulence within the command" that had resulted in "a general downgrade trend."[16] After his first year of command, the battalion's performance resulted in ARADCOM "E" Award for excellence in combat proficiency for all five battalion units. In 1966 the Key West Defense was the only one in the continental United States to win the award for all of its batteries.[17]

Our fourth baby was due to arrive just as Hurricane Inez made for Key West. We were living just yards away from the ocean with sliding glass doors facing the water. Joe and the children were evacuated to his headquarters, located in the old Casa Marina Hotel built in the 1920s by the railroad baron Henry Flagler, but I was sent to the hospital because I was already overdue to deliver the baby. The poor dog had to remain in the boarded up house overnight.

My doctor was so sympathetic about me being separated from my family that he graciously allowed me to stay in the staff quarters at Boca Chica Naval Air Station Hospital until Lucy Anne Muckerman, 9 pounds, 9 ounces, was born. She was our little "conch." Her brothers and big sister were delighted with this new baby. Later Martha made Lucy a funny little bathing suit and they loved taking her for a swim.

Joe with Hawk Missiles in Florida.

Whenever visiting dignitaries came to the area, Joe took them out on deep sea fishing trips and he was always giving talks. He joined the Key West Rotary. Joe was extremely well liked in Key West, and his ability to achieve results through sincere interest and charm were never more evident. Joe wrote that one trait that he inherited from his Gram was talking to strangers. Given a short period of time in any place, Joe knew dozens of people by their first names. Our friend Bill Kroll who owned "The Conch Train" asked him if he was going to run for mayor.

During our time in Key West Joe was able to save the iconic Conch Train Tour. It was in danger of being shut down due to the proximity of the train's path to the military base and the installation of the HAWK missiles. Joe cleared the train for approval to continue its tours, saving Bill Kroll's business as well as a long tradition that continues today. We made a return trip to Key West in 2006 with Lucy and her family, walking the familiar streets, riding the Conch Train, and enjoying lunch at the Casa Marina, now a beautifully restored Waldorf Astoria Resort.[18]

During this posting, Joe was instrumental in memorializing four local men who had died in Vietnam. On May 28, 1967, the *Key West Citizen* reported, "Thanks in part to Col. Muckerman, the names of four Key West men killed in Vietnam will live on as designations of local missile sites. All four men served in the U.S. Army." And on June 13, 1967, that newspaper published a farewell tribute at the end of Joe's command. Earlier in the year Joe had received the announcement of his selection to the Army War College, class of 1968.

Joe assuming command of 6th Hawk Missile Battalion.

War College—Carlisle, Pennsylvania

The U. S. Army War College is a center of higher education for Army officers who have been selected for higher leadership. Only a small percentage of all eligible officers are chosen to attend. The school's current website provides this description of their mission:

"The U.S. Army War College (USAWC) is the Army's ultimate professional development institution that prepares selected military, civilian, and international leaders for the responsibilities of strategic leadership in a joint, interagency, intergovernmental, and multinational environment. While it is primarily an institution run by and for the Army, officers from other branches

of U.S. Service and international participants are brought together for theoretical learning and strategical planning."

Ed and Pete practice saluting, just yards from our home.

When we arrived at Carlisle Barracks in Pennsylvania in the summer of 1967, we expected to be there for the ten months that Joe would be enrolled in the Army War College. We stayed three years, the longest time we had spent in one place for a long time. It had been hard to leave the little paradise that we had in Key West, but Carlisle allowed us to be closer to our families and we immediately liked the community and the opportunities for our children.

Our housing situation there was novel. Because of the ages and mix of our children, we were allowed two apartments that joined together. Lucy's crib and room were set up in the kitchen of the second apartment.

Joe's Academic Report dated June 10, 1968, cites consistent preparation, high level participation, effective communication of his ideas, and his ability to work with others. Noted as "above average in comparison with his War College classmates" were his writing skills. In spite of the rater's comment that Joe's verbal communication skills "lack the sparkle of dynamism (sic) that would enhance receptivity due to his quiet and reserved nature," he was recommended as a potential instructor in the Department of Strategy.[19]

At home in Key West: L to R, Peter, Anne, Lucy, Ed, Joe, Martha.

Possibly it was recognized that Joe's reluctance for self-promotion of his own ideas was a quality that leant itself well to instructing other officers. Joe was invited to remain at the War College as Director of Communist Military Strategy Studies. I think that it was during this time that he really honed his writing skills and developed what others often cited as his ability to both discern the important features of a problem and distill masses of information into workable solutions.

In a letter to me, our friend Howard Jelinek, who was sponsored and recommended to the faculty by Joe, recalled, "Joe was the finest War College instructor that I have ever known. For me to replace him as an instructor was a challenge. Fortunately, Joe left a great deal of material and information on his desk and every day I would uncover some of his military strategy concepts and ideas that would add value to the seminars." Howard also recalled that Joe enjoyed going for morning runs long before recreational running became popular. "Joe was ahead of his time in so many ways…and he was as knowledgeable as he was soft spoken."[20]

In the Performance Review ending June 1969, at the end of his first teaching year, Joe's department head at the Department of Strategy wrote, "He is a completely dedicated officer who is devoted to pursuit of excellence. His quiet demeanor is deceptive because in conducting seminars, he comes up with just the right observation or precisely the pertinent question to achieve outstanding results, the impact of which is magnified by his use of a low-key approach."[21]

After daughter Martha became interested in joining the Girl Scouts, I too became very involved as the Area Director in charge of seven troops. It was a big job coordinating activities and banquets and fundraisers and, of course, cookie sales, all out of our own building. This was hard work with two little boys who had different interests and three-year-old Lucy in tow, but we had a lot of fun. We borrowed equipment and went camping at Fort Miles in Delaware. Another time I organized a drive to save Betty Crocker coupons that we were able to redeem for 100 place settings of stainless flatware. Unfortunately we had to leave before I was able to find a successor. Through the years all four of the children had their turns at scouting with Ed staying in the longest and becoming an Eagle Scout; a very proud moment for Joe and me.

I became involved in the International Cooking Group too. Every month a handful of us would cook lunch for the group at one of the houses—I gathered a great collection of recipes in the process. It was in Carlisle that we first became interested in antiques. The area had many dealers and Joe and I liked nothing more than driving around the countryside and nosing through shops and dusty barns to uncover all manner of treasures.

Joe was promoted to Colonel while we were in Carlisle, and at the end of his second year on the faculty he received his next assignment, which would take us to California.

After the close of the school year, we all spent a wonderful summer at Eagles Mere in the eastern mountains of Pennsylvania. We stayed in a great resort area where we took hikes in the gorgeous Pocono Mountains and my mother did a lot of painting. We ate all of our meals in the hotel and at night there would be movies, shows, and various forms of entertainment. The older children ran to eat when the first dinner bell rang, then hurried back to take charge of Lucy and allow the adults to go to dinner. This gave them great license. One evening Ed came back to tell that he had ordered "halibut steak" thinking it was beef. They also ordered lemon juice in the morning and promptly dumped the contents of the sugar bowl into their glasses.

Fort MacArthur, San Pedro, California.

Fort MacArthur was established in 1914 for defense of the Los Angeles harbor. By the 1950s it was charged with responsibility for the air defense of the entire metropolitan Los Angeles area.

California was a different world and Joe's career

was really on a roll! Ft. MacArthur was a nice, small post with tennis courts and a swimming pool, both located a short distance from our quarters. We occupied Quarters One, a California mission revival style stucco house with a tile roof and a large porch. The houses on Officer's Row overlooked the parade field and tall palms were planted in rows along all of the streets.

Joe was named Commanding Officer of the 19th Artillery Group which included eight batteries located within a 25,000 square mile area, three with nuclear-capable Nike Hercules missiles. From 1950-1974, Fort MacArthur was part of the Nike surface-to-air defense system. Missile launch sites were located in areas surrounding Los Angeles—in the San Gabriel Mountains to the north and the Whittier Hills to the east—and administered through Fort MacArthur. One of Joe's great thrills during this assignment came from the regular helicopter transportation that flew him between the batteries and around the Los Angeles Harbor.

For safety and security reasons, the Nike Hercules missiles were stored in underground bunkers, most in very remote areas. This sometimes caused public relations problems with expanding suburban development. Acting as the face of the Army before a civilian population had always been a talent of Joe's. He often attended civic association gatherings and made many friends. He also had to maintain the morale of his troops, men who stood long shifts in lonely locations balancing the tedium of long periods of expectant waiting with the potential of nuclear attack.[22]

In the late summer of 1970 wildfire wreaked havoc on many locations in hills around Los Angeles, destroying hundreds of thousands of acres and many structures. At the end of September, brush fires were moving dangerously close to several of the 65th Artillery's batteries. At one critical point communication between the batteries and Fort MacArthur was completely cut off. The expression "brush fire" sounds somewhat tame but the burning underbrush was rolling like liquid over the steep hillsides and igniting tall trees that would explode like rockets from the internal heat. Between the falling debris and the unpredictable paths of these fires, the danger to the firefighters was enormous. County firefighters were well trained to handle large fires but the number of individual fires threatened to overwhelm them and their equipment. California counted 56 major blazes in four days ranging from Sequoia to San Diego and charring nearly half a million acres.[23]

Army missilemen and other post volunteers formed the first line of defense against the fires that approached their batteries. Subsequently they received reinforcement from county and civilian firefighters. Working together they managed to control the fires before damage occurred to any of the missile launch sites, and no one was seriously injured. When the crisis was past, Joe declared a Special Day of Thanksgiving for Sunday, October 4, 1970. In his address he said,

> "We can be grateful that not a member of this defense was lost or injured. Also, we can be grateful for the splendid spirit of cooperation and teamwork displayed by members of this command...The successful safeguarding of lives and equipment was indeed a marvelous achievement, if not a miraculous one. In view of these blessings, let each of us take time this Sunday to give thanks to Divine Providence."[24]

Since his command demanded that he move constantly around the Los Angeles area, Joe also had a personal driver, Daniel Frank, assigned to him. This was a convenience and a privilege that Joe enjoyed, but it was a perk he was determined not to abuse. Writing to me after Joe had died, Dan Frank recalled that Joe often asked him to stop the car so that he could get out to walk. This was a sign to Dan that Joe needed time and space to think something out. Dan would follow at a discreet distance or park until Joe reappeared and was ready to move on.

In 2011, when Dan wrote to me that "Col. Muckerman was an amazing man who cared about his men, who led by example, and honored his country with his service," I had already received the microfilm records from the Army that included thirty years of Joe's Performance Reports and I was immediately struck by the similarity of Dan's tribute to what was written about Joe by his Rating Officer in Japan, Major Ralph G. Duncan, over 60 years earlier:

Quarters One at Fort MacArthur.

> "Physically, mentally and morally, this officer is of the highest caliber. He is an asset and a credit to the service, When duty required extra long hours he performed all of his duties conscientiously, efficiently and in a cheerful manner. His manner of utilizing manpower is superior. He is a strong leader of men. He sets an example to those under him which results

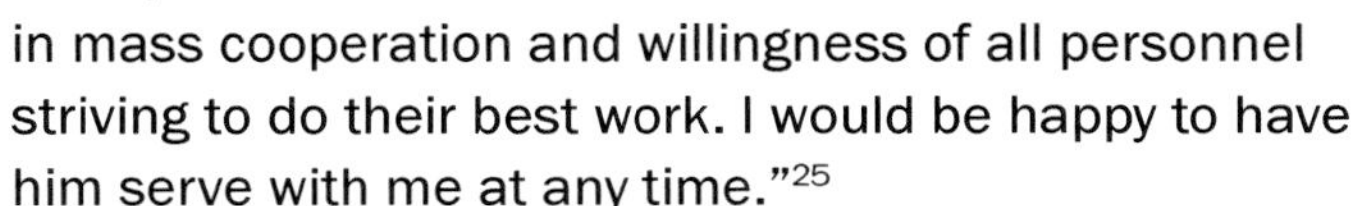

> in mass cooperation and willingness of all personnel striving to do their best work. I would be happy to have him serve with me at any time."[25]

In April 1971 the *Military Review*, the professional journal of the U.S. Army, published Joe's article, "Bay of Pigs Revisited." Written during the Vietnam War and the period of national conflict about that war, Joe addresses the inevitability of more Vietnams, but reflects on important lessons that could be learned from the Cuban Crisis in determining future U.S. involvements in external conflicts. "Bay of Pigs Revisited" was later selected as a "Military Review Award Article." [26]

Our street at Fort MacArthur.

As we were preparing to leave California, Joe was awarded the Legion of Merit (First Oak Leaf Cluster) "for exceptionally meritorious conduct in the performance of outstanding services." Joe had become expert in bringing posts under his command up to very high standards and achieving the highest ARADCOM ratings.

It was also a closing of sorts for us. Fort MacArthur would be our last Army Fort assignment. Since our marriage in 1953, Joe had been assigned to ten different locations (including two assignments that required me to move back to Alexandria with the children to be close to my mother. Our civilian friends are always surprised to hear that we never considered this a sacrifice. The greatest hardship was being separated from Joe. We loved every place we were posted; it was always an adventure.

(L to R) Peter, Lucy, Martha and Ed on our porch at Fort MacArthur in 1972.

There was a special esprit de corps among the Army families. We could arrive on a Monday and by the following Wednesday I would be attending a welcoming luncheon and our children would have already established playmates within an easy walking distance of our new home. Often they would find themselves reunited with friends from previous postings. Our communities were safe and clean and the schools were well equipped to integrate new students. We had a strong sense of equality because we were all living at similar pay grades and were housed with families of similar rank. I could not pick out a favorite place because each evokes special memories and wonderful friendships.

In those days wives did not often work outside of the home, so our careers were an extension of our husbands' careers. I was not without obligations. Each place we lived had a social decorum and a network of women who supported each other and their young families. We felt that our children had the best of both worlds. Like us, they enjoyed their friendships but learned to take the small problems in stride because they knew they would be moving on. If things became too routine, they would look forward to where we might go next. However, with four children living in somewhat close quarters at times, they had to work out their sibling issues. Playmates would change but brothers and sisters learned to get along regardless of where we lived.

When Joe received orders for the Pentagon in October 1971, we would finally put down roots.

The Pentagon

Headquarters of the Department of Defense.

Pentagon Army Staff to the Office of the Deputy Chief of Staff for Military Operations.

Office of J5 – Plans & Policy.

Since we had lived our entire married life with the constant need to move quickly when the Army told us to, we had always preferred to be renters. With this move we both realized that it was time to settle down and buy a house. Many of the friends Joe made in the Army over the past 25 years had ended up in the Washington area, my mother was living in Old Town Alexandria, and my sisters Judy and Sissy and their families were in the area, too. It felt like a homecoming.

I was still packing up in California when Joe flew to Washington in October 1971. He took the opportunity to go house hunting, and I sent my mother along for backup. I wanted to live in the Belle Haven subdivision of Alexandria where we had rented the darling house where I had lived with Martha, Ed, and Peter while Joe was in Vietnam. It had remained a congenial neighborhood with many children and it was located directly across from Belle Haven Country Club, an ideal place for our family of four active children who loved to swim. When the real estate agent asked him what price range we were looking for, Joe said "$32,000." After spending one day looking at houses in that range, Joe decided, "Maybe we'd better up the price." After that adjustment, they found the perfect house where we would live for 36 years. Purchase price: $62,000.

As happy as we had been moving around, we now were enjoying all the advantages of putting down roots. Joe served as President of the Belle Haven Association for a busy year and for a different year I was President of the Belle Haven Women's Club. Ed became an Eagle Scout—how proud we were of him! All of our children went to Camp Seafarer and Camp Seagull in North Carolina during the summers. We visited Joe's parents who were then in Colorado along with his sister Mary Ann and her husband Jack and their children. We always had a wonderful time in Estes Park and later in Steamboat Springs and Boulder.

On Sunday evenings we all loved to go to my mother's house for dinner. Once she cooked tongue in the crock pot. It tasted like corned beef. When the children found out they were horrified, and to this day one of them is likely to question the contents when they see that I am cooking with my crock pot.

Peter gave us a big scare in the spring of 1972. He came home from school with a note from the school nurse saying he should see the eye doctor. I made an appointment for about a month away. During the appointment the doctor spent a long time looking at Peter's eye before referring him to a specialist. Another month passed waiting for that appointment. Then that doctor spent an inordinate amount of time before declaring, "I'm making an emergency appointment for tomorrow morning at Walter Reed Hospital," and out we went in fear and trepidation. The next morning an entire team of doctors examined our scared little boy, including Dr. Beauchamp, who is now a renowned eye surgeon. Peter was admitted and operated on for a detached retina. The doctors were very upset that it took so long to get into Walter Reed and told us Peter could have gone blind at any time. They kept asking him if he had any traumas or injury to his head. Eventually Peter said that he was hit in the eye by a fastball on the tennis courts.

Typically each of our kids went through a period when they would rather "sleep in" than go to Sunday Mass. Joe laid the law down and said that as long as they were living at "2103" they were expected to go to church. For a while we went to Sunday Mass with a dear neighbor, Marge Haley. She had a huge

Cadillac that she called "The Queen Mary." Marge always wanted Joe to drive the car as she was getting up in years. She had a great sense of humor and we laughed all the way to church and all the way home. We used to sit on the side pews at church and we called it "casualty corner" because all the people had canes or crutches. One time we went to the Vigil Mass the night before Easter and it turned out being about two and a half hours long. Marge remarked that she was about to lose her religion.

When we moved to Belle Haven, daughter Martha had entered her senior year in high school. It was hardest on her to begin a new school—she attended four different schools in four years—but she made the most of it. Each of our children, in their turn, graduated from high school and went on to college.

For three and a half years Joe worked long hours in the Pentagon in the Strategy and Forces Division of the Organization of the Joint Chiefs of Staff (in official shorthand: OJCS – J-5). During the winter months it was barely light when he left in the mornings and dark when he came home, but he loved it all. He was repeatedly recognized for his contributions in evaluating highly technical information and interpreting the interdependence between the different branches of the military, his ability to work under extreme pressure, and the diplomacy required to bring members of various branches of the military together. In March 1973 he received the Meritorious Service Medal (First Oak Leaf Cluster) for his contributions during the period of December 1971 through March 15, 1973 and was named Deputy Head of the Strategy and Forces Division of the Office of the Joint Chief of Staff. In January 1974 Joe received a Letter of Commendation for service to the Joint Chiefs for his detailed and thorough work on a Joint

Our home in Alexandria, Virginia.

Strategic Objectives Plan. In January 1976 he received another Meritorious Service Medal (Second Oak Leaf Cluster).

The best description of Joe's work appears in the final performance report[27] for the period ending July 1975 and is signed by the Assistant Director, the Deputy Director, and the Lt. General John H. Elder, Jr., Director for Plans and Policy of the Joint Chiefs of Staff,

Lucy with her cousin Paige Pohlers in 1972.

"As a member of the Joint Staff "think tank" Col. Muckerman's performance has been exemplary. He has been engaged in the evaluation of a number of complex and critical national security issues requiring clear and thorough analysis along with the generation of imaginative alternative solutions. Almost single-handedly he had conducted a broad, preliminary review of our basic military strategy with a view toward triggering a fundamental review at the national level. Prior to that effort he worked with a colleague in developing an in-depth report on US policy for the Middle East. This was accomplished under the press of time and the reality of actual crisis in that region. Col. Muckerman is a highly dedicated and sophisticated officer who is fully qualified for promotion."

– William Nicholson, III, BGEN, USAF Assistant Deputy Director for Force Development & Strategic Plans. OJCS.(27)

"Colonel Muckerman has applied his unique talents to proposing solutions to some of the most critical security issues facing our nation. The review of National strategy and review of Middle East policy referred to by the rater were major studies of significant importance to the JCS. As an officer of exceptional abilities and unlimited growth potential I recommend his promotion to Brigadier General."

-Robert Hilton, RADM, USN, Deputy Director for Force Development & Strategic Plans, OJCS [28]

Industrial College of the Armed Forces at the

National Defense University

In the final years of his Army career, Joe was assigned to teach at the Industrial College of the Armed Forces, National Defense University. The Defense University is a joint military training educational institution under the direction of the Chairman, Joint Chiefs of Staff. The Industrial College of the Armed Forces (ICAF) is a senior level college providing graduate level education to senior members of the US armed forces, government civilians, foreign nationals, and private industry.[29] Attendance at ICAF is the equivalent of graduate school for members of the military who are at a rank of Lt. Colonel, Commander, or higher, government civilians with a CS grade of 14 or higher, or private sector civilians with 20+ years of work experience.[30] Program graduates are awarded a master of science degree in national resource strategy.

Joe was a natural teacher who brought over 25 years of experience as a senior Army officer and as a member of the Plans & Policy Division supporting the Joint Chiefs of Staff. He had expertise in both command and management, experience teaching at the War College, and knowledge about nuclear weaponry and the complexities of strategic military planning. Still, this was not an appointment but a position for which he was required to interview.

At the end of a long formal interview with whom I believe was the department head, Joe was asked if he felt that his qualifications were strong enough, given that he did not have a master's degree. Joe replied, "That makes two of us, sir." And he was hired! When he told me this story I asked Joe if he didn't think his reply was a bit impertinent, but Joe answered that he had done his own homework before the interview and knew that the senior instructor didn't have the degree either. Joe's preparations and good humor were always among his arsenal of secret weapons.

Beginning as a faculty member at ICAF, he quickly moved to head of Defense Programs Group. In July 1979 Joe received the Defense Service Medal for "superior service as a faculty member, and subsequently, as Head of Defense Programs Group." I have uncovered many letters in Joe's files from students who wrote to compliment him and thank him for the quality of the courses he instructed and for his encouragement.

Our daughter Lucy recalls talking with Joe about his teaching style which encouraged all of his students to participate. If there was a quiet student he would make a point of asking for his opinion, always praising some element of the input in order to build the student's confidence and foster more participation. According to Lucy, Dad would try to build people up, not tear them down. As his own father, "E.C.," taught him, 'You can learn something new from everyone you meet.'"

In July 1976, in a rating report, Joe's department head, Col. Laurence Randall, and Major General Theodore Antonelli, the Commandant of the Industrial College, recommended Joe for promotion and return to the Department of Defense as a "top defense manager." General Antonelli wrote, "Colonel Muckerman is a truly outstanding instructor. He is highly intelligent, urbane and has exceptionally good judgment and a sense of proportions. He is one of those rare individuals who recognizes and understands the 'parts' but never loses sight and perspective of the 'whole.' He is held in great esteem by his peers and by the students. He has displayed initiative and drive of the highest order. Definitely General Officer caliber." [31]

I never understood why Joe was not promoted to Brigadier General. He loved his work and received much recognition by way of awards, medals, and citations through the years. After his death when I obtained the copies of the Performance Reports, I read that he was repeatedly recommended for promotion above the rank of Colonel. Why this didn't occur, I do not know. I suspect that Joe did, but he never spoke of it to me nor did it ever compromise his enthusiasm for his work.

Joe and I soon got into the habit of late dinners since we would both arrive home at around the same time. This was always a special time for us to catch up on each other's day and talk about our children—all of them following different interests and careers. We always respected each other's interests even when we didn't necessarily share them, but our family life was always the most important aspect of our lives.

In an effort to lose 40 pounds that had crept on over the years, I joined Weight Watchers. After achieving my weight loss goal, Weight Watchers invited me to work with them. I thought it over and I decided to do it. This was my first paying job since I lived in St. Louis before our marriage. I spent 26 years working for Weight Watchers and during that time remained busy and happy making so many nice friends. But it was my volunteer job at the Ft. Myer Thrift Shop that became my favorite thing to do and created an interest that Joe and I would later pick up in retirement. I worked with many interesting ladies there—Dossie Goodpaster, Pat Groves, Maryanne LeVan, Susan Christman, and many others.

In August 1979, after 30 years of Army service, Joe had reached the mandatory retirement requirement. Had it been up to him, I don't think he would have ever left the Army. In many ways, he never did.

L to R: Martha Ferguson Butler, Anne Muckerman, Judy Pohlers, Sissy and Nicky von Guggenberg, Henry Butler.

Chapter Five

Still Serving

Joe had his resumé prepared well in advance of his official retirement date of August 1, 1979. At 53, he was too passionate about government and too young to consider a slower pace.

After three and a half years as a project manager and analyst for the General Research Corporation in McLean, Virginia, where he was responsible for studies on industrial mobilization preparedness, the readiness of Reserve units, NATO logistics, and a range of related topics that were his specialty, Joe returned to the National Defense University at the Mobilization Concepts Development Center (MCDC) in April, 1982. His first job title was Senior Fellow, but as was his established course of advancement, he left in 1985 as its Director.

From a booklet put out by the MCDC during Joe's tenure:

> "The Mobilization Concepts Development Center is a specialized research and policy organization which operates under the direction of the President of the University. The Center provides intellectual and analytical resources to the Secretary and Deputy Secretary of Defense, Chairman, Join Chiefs of Staff, the Commanders in Chief, military Services and Executive Branch departments and agencies on a

broad spectrum of issues related to mobilization, deployment and industrial preparedness planning. The Center staff conducts derivative and original research and provides consultation on policy matters and issues of major concern to mobilization practitioners and war planners."

In Joe's own resumé of his job at MCDC, his responsibilities included designing and writing original plans, while analyzing and often blending strategic plans authored by other specialists in military, government, academics, and the private industrial sectors. Moreover, he was charged with bringing these specialists together in forums with the goal of a cooperative effort to design and prepare joint mobilization plans between Department of Defense and other Federal agencies.

Most likely as a result of national opinion in the years following American involvement in Vietnam, the focus on national defense in general, and the specific role of mobilization planning, had been significantly downplayed over several past presidential administrations. Then a shift occurred when Ronald Reagan assumed the presidency of the United States in 1981. One of the goals of the Reagan administration was to strengthen national defense. President Reagan selected Casper Weinberger as his Secretary of Defense. "Weinberger shared the President's conviction that the Soviet Union posed a serious threat and that the establishment needed to be modernized and strengthened...at the Pentagon Weinberger became a vigorous advocate of Reagan's plan to increase the Department of Defense budget. Readiness, sustainability, and modernization became the watchwords of the defense program."[1]

Joe and Craig Alderman.

A civilian position in the Pentagon reporting to Craig Alderman, Under Secretary of Defense for Policy, became available to Joe in 1986. The role of the Under Secretary is to assist in shaping the overall national security strategy. Alderman's own position had required a presidential appointment with Senate confirmation. The position that Joe would assume as Director of Emergency Planning was a presidential appointment, but not one requiring Senate confirmation. With this appointment Joe became a member of the elite Senior Executive Service (SES), serving in the key support positions just below the top Presidential appointees.

Joe's official job description:

> Mr. Muckerman, Director of Emergency Planning, Office of the Secretary of Defense. In this capacity, he serves as the principal assistant to the Deputy Under Secretary of Defense (Security Policy) in all areas relating to policies and requirements associated with national emergencies, emergency preparedness, civil defense, and concomitant matters. Specific responsibilities include the establishment of policy and requirements for the support of emergency preparedness, national emergency planning, military mobilization, industrial mobilization, civil defense, crisis management, and DOD participation in exercises.

In civilian terms, Joe was involved in peacetime planning for the eventuality of war. Overall, he coordinated what are broadly described as continuity of government programs. His work centered on developing programs and procedures for preserving the government and keeping it functional in the event of a national emergency or war. This was highly classified work that included the establishment of secure procedures for moving top government leaders to safe locations, keeping communication open to run the U.S. Government, and moving necessary materiel and supplies in times of natural crisis or enemy attack.

Joe's major emphasis was on the resources—men and materiel—needed to wage America's wars. He felt that there was insufficient attention paid to this aspect of preparedness. A colleague and friend, Col. (ret.) John Brinkerhoff, recalled that Joe liked to point out that when the experience of World War II was codified in the National Security Act of 1947, it provided, among other things, for a National Security Resources Board, as well as a Department of Defense, a separate Air Force, a Central Intelligence Agency, and other agencies. Joe noted that, alone among these new organizations, the one devoted to resources was not carried out.[2]

In addition to establishing a mobilization program in the Department of Defense and supporting preparedness measures, Joe also established a good relationship with the Federal Emergency Management Agency (FEMA), which was then responsible for National Mobilization Planning. He was a close friend and colleague with Joe Moreland, the senior FEMA official in charge of mobilization preparedness. The two Joes worked together and travelled together to explain and advocate preparedness. They supported the Global War Games conducted each summer by Bud Hay at the Naval War College. They participated in the activities of the War Resources Working Group (WRWG) that met quarterly to prepare for the resources aspects of the Global War Games. The WRWG meetings assembled senior officials from all federal departments and senior executives from many large defense contractors and suppliers to consider what needed to be done to provide the means to win the Cold War.[3]

One of Joe's most important contributions to mobilization preparedness was the concept of Graduation Mobilization Response (GMR). He invented and obtained approval for a new way of conducting mobilizations that could be started, stopped, and reversed if appropriate. This idea of planning a mobilization that could be flexible made it possible to avoid the dangers of previous plans that once started could not be stopped or reversed even when that would be necessary. Due to Joe's efforts, GNR became the official method for mobilization preparedness.[4]

Toward this goal, Joe was responsible for establishing the necessary interface with 27 other departments and agencies within the Federal government. Walking between different members of the Joint Chiefs, some of whom were career military and others political appointees, required a particular degree of finesse and diplomacy that Joe managed with relative ease, in part due to his temperament but mainly because he had earned a reputation for putting the success of a project above personal recognition.

A Department of Defense colleague, Colonel (ret.) David Garner, headed the Mobilization Plans branch on the Joint Staff and worked closely with Joe for three years. Writing about this in 2012, he recalls some of those unique qualities of Joe's personality and approach to encourage disparate personalities to work toward a common goal.

> Joe Muckerman was the consummate Christian gentleman. In every situation I ever observed Joe, he was considerate, patient, understanding, and one who sought to bring out the best in everyone and to bring "light, not heat" to every endeavor. His low-key (but very effective) approach contrasted with his passionate determination to improve our nation's security and preparednes... We could be in contentious meetings together, but Joe was unflappable; his quiet demeanor reflected a steadfastness of character that was evident to all with whom he interacted... We shared the same outlook, which he certainly fostered in me, that there was only one special interest in our work and that was the 'national interest.'

Beginning at the Military Academy through the Cold War and Vietnam, serving as commandant over Army installations that maintained watch over strategic areas on two coasts, over 40 years of experience stood behind Joe's conviction that our nation must be adequately prepared for emergencies, the most critical being hostile aggression leading to war. Soon our country would be facing both natural disasters and foreign enemies we hadn't even considered in the mid-1980s. Regardless of where the threats came from, Joe's experience and instincts about preparedness would be proven correct.

Due to the classified nature of his work, whatever

the problems were, he did not bring them home. I think I have learned more about his work through the research for this book than I ever knew before. Even in the years when his job at the Pentagon intersected with daughter Lucy's at the White House and they commuted together, Lucy remembers being the focus of her father's interest during their morning drives into Washington. This was always characteristic of Joe. He would focus on who he was speaking with to learn more about that person's interests and opinions. It was more than a need to deflect questions about himself or the classified logistics he was involved with; he had a genuine interest in people and a reticence about self-promotion. Joe could be forceful about his convictions while remaining modest about his achievements.

In the first edition of his book, *Assignment Pentagon, The Insider's Guide To The Potomac Puzzle Palace,* Major General Perry M. Smith includes Joe in the chapter, "People Who Can Help You." Perry writes, "Some names...of people who are especially well known for their understanding of Pentagon issues, for their willingness to share their insights, and for their longevity in important positions in the Building."[5]

Joe was highly thought of by his employees.

Joe remained at the Department of Defense until the end of 1992. As Lucy remembers her father telling her, all presidential appointees were to submit their resignations once the 1988 elections took place. Joe never got the word that he was to be replaced, so he continued on. Considering that the new president, George H. W. Bush, was also a Republican and retained many Republican staff appointees of his predecessor, this may have been business as usual and not a lapse of protocol. Nonetheless, Joe was happy to stay. However, in November 1992 with the election of President William Clinton, a Democrat, Joe would almost certainly have been asked to resign his presidential appointment. At 66 years young and full of good health, his thoughts were turning to a life outside of government employment.

At his final retirement party in December, colleagues presented Joe with several books intended for good wishes for him on the occasion of his second retirement. Repeatedly these pages are filled with handwritten sentiments to "the best boss I ever had" and bear heartfelt testimony to Joe's mentoring, career support, and friendship. Somewhere in this huge government installation they had found a unique place where they reported to work for a man who showed them personal concern and inspired them to feel that their contribution mattered.

> "I've never worked for anyone like you and I think you are probably the most loved boss in the Pentagon."
>
> "As long as public policy involves interpersonal coordination, you will be remembered for a lasting contribution on how to get along with people, while slowly but determinedly moving them toward the goal at hand."
>
> "I promise that we will attempt to carry out the course that you set for us – a sustainable graduated response to any crisis that challenges our national security."
>
> "You are a man of great strength and moral character and the DOD is impoverished because of your retirement."
>
> "It was a great honor to work with you... your lifelong devotion to your country was an inspiration to us all."

Back row: Joe Muckerman, Bob Ennis, Dan McGurk, Tim Cronin, Bill Earthman, Ed Yellman, Dick Bowman.

Front row: Anne Muckerman, Wren Ennis, Shirley McGurk, Jeannine Cronin, Dorothy Earthman, Eunice Yellman, Lois Bowman.

To really understand Joe is to know that he walked in concert with his Catholicism and love of God. This belief in being part of a much bigger plan and following the examples set forth by Jesus were intricately linked to his love of our family and to his service to our country. Joe was never a man for whom Sunday mass was an exoneration for what occurred the rest of the week; it was a celebration and time for renewing his core beliefs. To that, Lucy adds that it was very important to her father that his children practiced the lessons of faith by attending Mass every Sunday and by integrating those lessons into their daily lives—living their faith and knowing God.

Joe held very high standards for himself. This sometimes resulted in his being greatly disappointed by the underperformance or by the moral weakness of others. What distinguished Joe was that he did not sit in judgment of the personal frailties of others, with the possible exception of vainglorious leaders or duplicitous politicians whose egos interfered with their ability to perform honestly or competently. Our daughters Martha and Lucy both say that they never remember their father being openly critical of anyone. He would often remind them that they should be tolerant because they did not know someone's whole story or what that person might be going through at the time.

As his West Point classmate Dan McGurk remembered almost 60 years later, "I loved Joe. He was the nicest man I ever knew. He exuded good feelings and warmth. Not only was he quite religious (although he didn't flaunt it), but he was clearly gentle—both as a human being and also as a gentleman."

After his death, we found this undated but signed piece among Joe's personal papers.

HOLY MASS: A REFLECTION

By Joseph E. Muckerman II

The Pentagon is a huge building. It has about 23 miles of corridors and is divided into 4000 rooms. In one of the larger rooms on the 5th floor—A Ring—Holy Mass is celebrated each weekday at noon.

Thus during three separate tours of duty in the big building, I was able to attend Holy Mass frequently.

As the years passed, I began to piece together some thoughts on the Mass—its beauty and its meaning in terms of its relationship to our lives and our salvation. What follows in an attempt to express these thoughts.

Attendance at Mass is the most important act of worship for the Catholic. The Mass is at the very core of our religion. But what is the Mass? For many years I believed that it was simply the reenactment of the Last Supper and Calvary—God the Son offering Himself to God the Father for man's salvation.

But is that all Jesus Christ meant when He said—"Do this in memory of me"? What should we do at Mass beyond commemorating what Christ did for us? The answer it seems to me is that we should offer our lives to God, just as He offered Himself for us.

Each person born to this earth suffers and sacrifices—gives of him or herself. We have little control over what suffering befalls our lives, but the extent to which we give of ourselves for the good of others is our free choice. There are literally an infinite number of ways of giving or sacrificing our well being, needs, treasures, time, and pleasure for the good of others—family, friends, or strangers.

There are the big sacrifices which are associated with our chosen vocations, but within the framework of those vocations, there are an infinite number of smaller sacrifices that one can make on a daily basis—caring for a sick child, parent, or the needy, holding one's temper in the face of provocation, suppressing our desires and wishes to accommodate others, and on and on.

The key point is that we all give of ourselves—some in great measure over large spans of time, others, being self-centered, hardly at all.

On Calvary Jesus Christ gave everything so that we might be saved—His dignity, and His life down to His last drop of blood. That total sacrifice, which man can approach with God's grace, but never fully equal, should be our life's goal. And frequent attendance at Mass is the key and essential requirement for achieving that goal. The more often that we receive His Body and Blood at Holy Mass, the more that we will be able to give of ourselves in both large and small ways.

At the Offertory and again at the Consecration, we should offer our life and what we do with it during our lifetime to God for the well being and salvation of others. In so doing, we become Christ like because we do what He did. We follow in His footsteps.

This is what I believe Jesus Christ meant when He said, "Do this in memory of Me."

Chapter Six

A Little House by the Bay

Through the years we always loved going to the beach. Joe was fond of saying that he liked the mountains but he loved the water. Living in Virginia, we had access to the Virginia beaches, Delaware beaches, and the Eastern Shore, and over the years we enjoyed vacation time in all of these places. By 1988, with all four of our children through college and two married, Joe and I found a wonderful little house in Lewes, Delaware. After patiently waiting for the price to drop, we bought it. We had many happy times alone together or with friends, and, of course, with our children and growing battalion of grandchildren, but we continued to commute "home" to Belle Haven. When Joe retired from the Department of Defense at the end of 1992, I was still working with Weight Watchers and enjoying my friendships in Alexandria. Joe wanted to live fulltime in Lewes but I was not ready.

309 W. Third Street in Lewes, Delaware.

For Joe, retirement was not a cessation

of work, but an opportunity to continue on his own terms to pursue things that always interested him. He remained active with the professional community involved with mobilization and preparedness and was often asked to consult on aspects of national defense. In that capacity he became a consultant for defense policy for the Heritage Foundation, a conservative public policy research institution in Washington.[1]

Joe was also involved with the Association for National Defense and Emergency Resources (ANDER), an organization originally authorized by the Defense Production Act of 1950, but later renamed National Defense Executive Reserve (NDER) Program under the Federal Emergency Management Agency (FEMA) of the U.S. Department of Homeland Security. "ANDER is a Federal Government program that provides a reserve of highly qualified individuals from industry, organized labor, professional groups, and the academic community to serve in executive positions in the Federal Government in time of national emergency."[2] Working with his good friend Col. (ret.) Kay Kimura, Joe would follow Kay as President of ANDER.

Col. (ret.) John Brinkerhoff, former Associate Director of FEMA and an advocate of mobilization preparedness, remembers Joe's involvement and leadership in ANDER.

> Joe graciously hosted many meetings at the Belle Haven Country Club. He was able to obtain numerous senior officials, members of Congress, and leaders of industry to meet and discuss issues with the ANDER members. Along with other advocates of mobilization preparedness such as Dick Donnelly and myself, Joe donated his time and energy to visiting current and retired officials seeking to obtain support for reinstitution of the Nation Security Resources Board or a modern equivalent. He came to epitomize the need for the United States to be able to marshal the necessary resources that would be needed to assure national survival. [3]

These years also allowed for more time for large family trips and for grandparenting. Joe had no problem slipping from his role as a consultant on critical issues of mobilization preparedness to overseeing a passel of grandchildren. Parents still haven't invented adequate ways to be in more than one place at once, and at the Muckerman Emergncy Management Agency, Grandpa Joe was often commandeered into the familial branch of active duty.

We enjoyed active social contacts with the West Point alumni group in the Washington area and the friendship of our neighbors in Belle Haven and in Lewes. There was also more time for Joe to take walks, ride his bike, and sink into thousand-page histories that detailed military strategy, biographies of world leaders, and his favorite subject since boyhood, Pearl Harbor. Joe loved reading about all aspects of history. If we attended a cocktail party and he connected with a guest who had similar interests, Joe was content for the evening.

Our antique shop, Stack Arms.

In about 1994 we thought it might be fun to try a new joint adventure. We'd both spent a lot of time at local yard sales and I had considerable experience at the Ft. Myer Thrift Shop, so we took over a space in the Lewes Mercantile Antique Gallery on Second Street in Lewes. This was the beginning of our antique shop, "Stack Arms." It was great fun for both of us, and Joe would tell people that it gave me a good excuse to go on buying trips. He had a good eye too, and between us we uncovered fascinating treasures and turned a tidy profit. More than that, we had a mutual hobby and we met many interesting people through the years.

By 1997, during summer weekends the seams of our little cottage on Third Street in Lewes were straining with grandchildren. All of our children had married and we had been blessed through these marriages with daughters-in-law Toni and Stephanie, son-in-law Faron, and at that time seven grandchildren. Joe was increasingly lobbying for us to move to Lewes full time. Always the strategist, I think he knew that he would capture my interest when a larger house along the Lewes–Rehoboth Canal became available. He was right. Although it would require renovations, it had many features that made it perfect for us, including large fireplaces and a magnificent view of the canal and the wetlands. So, we took the plunge and bought it, choosing initially to rent it to a tenant until we had our plans in place.

We were living in two houses, working part time at our business in Lewes, and busy with plans for the house on the canal. Life did not lack variety. The two-and-a-half-hour drive from Alexandria to Lewes was beginning to wear us down, but once we parked our car in our driveway in Lewes we wouldn't get in it again until we left to go back to Virginia. We could walk or ride bikes wherever we needed to go in Lewes, and neighbors were all so friendly. Soon Joe became an easily recognized figure pedaling his old bike from Roosevelt Inlet to Cape Henlopen and all roads in between. He loved small town life. Just as he had done years before when we lived in Key West, he became the Lewes Town Booster, never tiring of extolling its many virtues. Like his beloved Gram, Annie Schmieder, there were no strangers to Joe, just people he hadn't met yet.

Joe had a wonderfully romantic side that some people might not associate with an Army colonel, but Joe always defied stereotyping. We often played music in the house while we sat together reading or tending to our chores. Often he would drop whatever he was doing, take my hand, and dance me around the living room. He especially loved the song, "Blue Spanish Eyes." Joe was always very thoughtful and observant. He might come home and present me with a gift-wrapped box containing a dress that I had admired in a shop window a week before. He had beautiful taste in both clothing and jewelry, but most endearing was the effort behind the gift. On our 40th anniversary in 1993 Joe adapted a fairly obscure poem for me.[4]

As bright your beauty still appears
As on our wedding day.
We will not care that spring be past
And autumn shadows fall;
These years shall be, although the last,
The loveliest of all.

These "retirement years" were everything we could have dreamed of. We watched from the sidelines while our children developed their interests and careers and raised families of their own. We were both so proud of each of them. As long as they were doing well, we were too.

Happiness seemed limitless and that was when Joe's worst fears came true.

Our continuing interest in our antiques business prompted us to join three specialized antique-buying trips with a company called Through The Looking Glass. We went to England twice and to France in 2001 on a barge trip. That was one of the most wonderful trips of our life—wonderful food, beautiful boat, interesting travelers, entertainment from Spanish guitar players, and land trips pre-arranged along the way. Most tragically, the end of the trip coincided with the September 11 terrorist attacks on Americans.

I can remember every detail of that day. We'd been having another remarkable day when in the middle of the afternoon, Debbie, our trip coordinator, called us into the lounge. With her voice trembling, she proceeded to tell us what had happened and that she hoped that none of our family members were affected. Having no television or phone access from the barge, Debbie made arrangements for us to go to a hotel in the town where we could watch the news via CNN. We all sat silently and in complete shock. Eventually some members of the group were able to make international cell phone connections to the States and another person obtained an American newspaper that each of us took turns devouring.

It was a Tuesday and we were not scheduled to leave France until the following Sunday. The French people were very concerned and compassionate toward us and we were much relieved to finally make telephone connections and learn that our families were safe, but the uncertainty of everything blanketed the rest of the trip. As it turned out, Joe's former offices in the Pentagon suffered a direct hit, but due to a reorganization that had taken place to facilitate upgrades to that section, most of his immediate colleagues were no longer occupying that area. Nonetheless, our grief as Americans and as part of the fellowship of Pentagon employees was immense.

For Joe, who had spent so many of his professional years preparing for a national emergency and arguing for a strong protective defense of the United States, there was certainly no victory in being right. Two months earlier *The New York Times* published an article by a former State Department counterterrorism specialist named Larry C. Johnson, titled "The Declining Terrorist Threat." A few days later in the Letters to the Editor section, Joe's letter appeared arguing against the relaxation of American vigilance against terror. In his closing paragraph, Joe wrote, "The attack on Pearl Harbor was successful because we, as a nation, had not crossed a mental threshold that admitted that our territory could be attacked. Let us not make that mistake again."[4]

We returned home from France and joined with all of America in this time of national mourning. Through the years many people have described their own experience hearing about the events on September 11, 2001, and living in the aftermath, as "surreal." For us, living in the metropolitan Washington area and often driving right by the Pentagon, it was very real. I think that knowing our children and grandchildren were safe, and focusing on keeping the world safe for them, reminded us that we had to live normally and in the present.

Chapter Seven

Who Could Ask for Anything More?

Joe and I celebrated our 50th wedding anniversary with a Wedding Renewal Mass at St. Mary's, our church in Alexandria, on October 11, 2003. Our children sent out beautiful invitations with our 1953 wedding photograph and arranged a reception afterwards at the Belle Haven Country Club. How had the years passed so quickly? How had we been so lucky?

Family portrait from 2003.
L to R: Lucy, Joe, Peter, Martha, Anne, Ed.

The following January in the *New York Times* Opinion section, a woman named Laura Kipnis wrote a piece, "The State of the Unions; Should This Marriage Be Saved?"[1] putting forth her opinions about the deteriorating state and antiquated value of marriage. Joe shot off a letter to the editor that appeared in the *New York Times* on February 1, 2004.

> Laura Kipness looks only at the negatives of matrimony...My wife and I recently celebrated our 50th wedding anniversary. The fruits of this union were four wonderful children and nine grandchildren, with one on the way. Certainly there were tough times—a year's separation during the Vietnam War, sickness, lots of homework, bad report cards, teenage rebellions and so on.
>
> But when we gathered to repeat our marriage vows last October, both of us were in total agreement that marriage can only be described as the divine architecture for achieving ultimate and true happiness.
>
> The tables have turned—we took good care of our children and now they take care of us. We kept our marriage vows and will reap our rewards until death do us part.
>
> – Joseph E. Muckerman II, Alexandria, Va.

Joe never hesitated to sharpen his pencil and send his opinions off to an editor or government representative. Other people had crossword puzzles to stimulate their brains; Joe had the entire first sections of the *Washington Post* and *The New York Times* and he never hesitated to exercise his right to verbally challenge government decisions or the press.

Joe and Anne at their 50th anniversary party.

A series of events in 2006 led to our decision to leave our home in Belle Haven. There was definitely a measure of sadness attached to our decision because we had loved this house and felt such a strong attachment to the neighborhood. Luckily we found the perfect family to take our place—our own children, Lucy and Faron, and their expanding family of daughters. Joe and I decided to move into an apartment in Alexandria until all the various pieces of our final move could fall into place. We became full-time residents of Lewes, Delaware, in March 2010, living in the house on the canal that we had also named "Stack Arms."

The previous year had been a difficult one. I had a series of health problems. Each one had been a mountain to climb, but we thought the final peak would be the completion of our move from Alexandria. Considering the constant stresses, Joe wasn't especially concerned about his various symptoms of indigestion. I worried about his weight loss, but he insisted that his doctor told him that his weight was perfect. Joe had been extremely careful about his diet since a diagnosis of high cholesterol years before, but age does challenge how we physically respond to change.

The winter of 2009-2010 had been the worst on record in our mid-Atlantic region and it seemed as if both the move and the unpredictable weather would never end. Joe's flu-like symptoms extended just as long. When spring finally came, Joe did not experience any relief. He finally confided to me that he thought that something was seriously wrong. In early June the worst was confirmed. Joe had a very advanced form of stomach cancer. When the doctor presented us with the diagnosis, Joe was the only calm person in the room. He broke the silence with, "Well, you have to die of something." Our children immediately set up a schedule to rotate their visits. We were never alone. Their outpouring of love for both of us carried me through what was unquestionably the worst time of my life.

After considering treatment options, the choice was made for palliative care and adjustments made to improve his comfort. While the rest of us stumbled around in a state of disbelief, Joe continued to set the tone for normalcy. He was pensive but never morose. There were things he needed to consider, conversations he wanted to have. One afternoon as he sat with our granddaughter Emily, he lifted the

Miraculous Medal that he always wore from around his neck and transferred it to hers. I'd given it to him before he left for Vietnam in 1964. The Miraculous Medal is a great testimony to faith and the power of trusting prayer. Its greatest miracles are those of patience, forgiveness, repentance, and faith.[2] It was time to pass it on.

During his last weeks, Joe was able to take a few more short rides on his beloved "Taxi" bike or watch the rose and gold sunsets from our dock on the canal where he savored the briny scent of the salt marsh. He was physically weak but free of pain and clear of mind. An article on June 19th in the *Washington Post* about our government's purchase of Russian helicopters for Afghanistan's air force drew his ire, prompting a letter to the editor. Complete with historical references to World War ll, it was published in the *Post* on June 21st.[3]

We had scheduled a business meeting on June 25th that was attended by all of the children and several others. It was a long meeting and assured Joe that all financial details of our estate had been completed. As the meeting concluded, Joe moved to the bedroom to rest. He awoke late that afternoon and talked with daughter Lucy who was sitting beside the bed. He was convinced that it was morning because he felt that he had been awakened by very bright light that he insisted was coming through our east-facing windows. He declined food, so Lucy urged him to close his eyes and rest some more. She said that she loved him and he replied, "I love you more than life itself." Lucy had no reason to know it then, but these words were his last.

St. Joseph was Joe's own patron saint and for all the years of our marriage Joe prayed to St. Joseph, keeping the same small, 10-cent book in his nightstand, "Prayers to Saint Joseph with Novena." St. Joseph is believed to intercede with God to bring a merciful or compassionate death. It was.

Father Jim from St. Jude's was called in the morning to deliver last rites. Hospice, still an intermittent presence, dispatched a nurse, also named Joe. His kindness and compassion will never be forgotten.

With all of us surrounding him, our Joe ascended from this life on June 26th.

Having such deep attachments to three different communities, I understood the importance of services that would allow our friends in each of these places to celebrate Joe's life. On Friday, July 9th, we celebrated the Funeral Mass at St. Mary's in Alexandria, Virginia. On Saturday, August 9th we held a Memorial Mass at St. Jude's in Lewes. And finally, on October 10, a most beautiful, warm autumn day, Joe was interred at Arlington National Cemetery with full military honors. In Spokane, our dear friend Father John McBride said a Mass for Joe and our family, timing it precisely as the funeral was to begin at Arlington.

Led by a police escort, the funeral motorcade made its way through Old Town Alexandria to the massive gates of Arlington National Cemetery. Waiting there, the honor guard, the flag bearers, the caparisoned horse, and the military band all stood at rapt attention as the soldiers first saluted, then carried the casket to the horse-drawn caisson. The ceremony proceeded in a precise but hushed manner as the caisson moved forward, followed by the honor guard, then the full dress Army band playing as they marched. We followed behind as they played the Alma Mater from West Point. Walking in perfect cadence, the soldiers lifted the casket and carried it to the burial spot.

Chairs had been arranged for us. The post chaplain said a few words followed by Deacon Bill Pyrek from the Lewes Church of St. Jude. In the distance a 21-gun salute was fired, and later the grandchildren were able to retrieve some of the spent shells for safekeeping. The soldiers presented me with the perfectly folded American flag that had covered the casket, and our friend June Todd, who was the official "Arlington Lady" for Joe's ceremony, joined me to express sympathy on behalf of the Joint Chiefs of Staff. Then came the mournful sound of "Taps" and Joe was laid to rest in Section 60, often referred to as "the saddest acre in America,"[4] ground he shares with the many young soldiers whose lives were taken in Afghanistan and Iraq. It was a most touching and unforgettable ceremony.

In a letter of counsel and comfort to me, our dear friend Father John McBride wrote that Joe will always be at my elbow. This is surely an expression that continues to bring a smile to me on so many occasions when I know that Joe is, and always will be, with me. Faith is not what we can see, but that which we believe.

In my faraway dreams I see Joe, so tall and handsome with his piercing blue eyes and wonderful smile. He folds me in his arms and tells me, "Be not afraid." His beautiful hands guide me along the path to Heaven with him.

When he shall die,
Take him and cut him out in little stars,
And he will make the face of heaven so fine
That all the world will be in love with night
And pay no worship to the garish sun.

-William Shakespeare,
From *Romeo and Juliet*

Chapter Eight

Tributes

Joseph E. Muckerman II '49

No. 17279 ■ 4 Jul 1926 – 26 Jun 2010 ■ Died in Lewes, DE
Interred in Arlington National Cemetery, Arlington, VA

"I loved Joe. He was the nicest man I ever knew. He exuded good feelings and warmth. Not only was he quite religious, although he didn't flaunt it, but he was clearly gentle; both as a human being and also as a gentleman." Joseph Edward Muckerman's classmate, Dan McGurk, accurately and succinctly expressed the feelings of Joe's Company M-2 classmates. Many who served with Joe in later years held similar views.

Joseph E. Muckerman II was born in St. Louis, MO, on 4 Jul 1926. His parents were Edward C. Muckerman and Josephine Muckerman. A sister, Mary Ann, came later. Joe attended Saint Louis University High School, a Jesuit institution, during 1940–44. When he announced he wanted to enlist, his father suggested he consider West Point. Joe enrolled in Millard Preparatory School and succeeded in getting appointed to West Point.

Most new cadets in 1945 were already in military service. Jim Lampros, Joe's Beast Barracks roommate, remembers Joe drawing disproportionate attention from upper classmen eager to improve his military bearing.

The end of World War II led to a reduced need for lieutenants and the Academy, grading on the curve, chopped away at the Class of 1949. Joe was under continuous pressure to stay ahead of the severing blade. Joe branched Artillery after graduation. His subsequent assignments were progressive and indicative of an officer on a fast track. During the Korean Conflict, 1LT Muckerman served in Japan as an acting anti-aircraft battery commander.

Mary Ann Muckerman's best friend in high school was Anne Butler. Joe and Anne became engaged just before Joe left for the Far East. They married in Ladue, MO, on his return in 1953. The couple reported to Ft. Sill, where Joe became battery executive, then S-3 of a 155 mm gun battalion and was promoted to captain.

Daughter Martha was born in December 1954. Joe was next assigned to the staff communications branch in the Pentagon. Son Edward was born in November 1957 in Alexandria, VA. In 1958, Joe found himself in Panama, commanding Battery C of the 517th Artillery. Son Peter was born in Panama in March 1960. Daughter Lucy was born in Key West in October 1966.

In mid-1961, Joe was promoted to major and entered the Command & General Staff College at Ft. Leavenworth. His critical thinking and communication skills led to a two-year assignment on the faculty. In October 1964, Joe went to Vietnam as a sector advisor with the 9th Vietnamese Division in Vinh Binh Province. He earned the Combat Infantryman Badge and the Vietnamese Cross of Gallantry and was promoted to lieutenant colonel. Joe returned from Vietnam to a critical assignment, commander of a Hawk missile battalion in Key West shortly after the Cuban Missile crisis. Defense of the continental U.S. remained a serious concern.

Joe next attended the Army War College and then spent two years on the faculty as director of Communist Studies. In July 1970, Joe assumed command of the 13th Artillery Group, defending the Los Angeles area in the era of mutually assured destruction. Joe had the key role, directing Army, Navy and Air Force elements in the defense of Los Angeles.In 1976, Joe was director, Communist Military Strategy Studies and director, Defense Programs Department for the Industrial College of the Armed Forces. His rapid progression testified to Joe's performance. However, Dan McGurk's insightful description of Joe Muckerman invites a question. Could someone who was "loveable, exuded good feelings, and clearly gentle perform well in the military?"

The answer, expressed by higher level officers:

"... loyal to superiors and well-liked by his subordinates."

"... reflected his competence, but also his essential decency."

"... Established a ... close working relationship with his Vietnamese counterparts and the Province chief ..." a relationship "not even approached by any other advisor."

"... without a doubt one of the best officers I have had the privilege to serve with."

"... most intelligent officer I have ever met."

"... represents the finest of army officers."

"... more closely approaches the theoretical officer in all respects, than any officer I have known."

Several of his superior officers commented on Joe's special talent: he could articulate concisely the central point that others may have missed. His October 1971 assignment to the office of the Joint Chiefs of Staff provided the ideal venue for his analytical, communication and leadership skills, where he contributed to or led study groups formulating the Army's strategic plans. Joe's principal assignment was deputy chief, Nuclear Forces and Policy Division. He was commended repeatedly and promoted to colonel in May 1974.

Joe retired from the Army in 1979 and joined General Research Corporation, a consulting firm focused on military issues. He later joined the Mobilization Concepts Development Center, National Defense University. MCDC advised the DOD on mobilization and industrial preparedness. Joe became director, Defense Programs Division.

In 1986, Joe returned to the Pentagon as a civilian director of emergency planning under the Secretary of Defense. He was repeatedly recognized for the quality of his contributions to the nation's readiness. He retired again in 1992.

Joe Muckerman, in Dan McGurk's words, was "quite religious." He attended daily Mass whenever he could.

Because he could get quickly to the heart of an issue and succinctly surface what others overlooked, the *New York Times* and the *Washington Post* published many of his letters. Longer articles on national strategy and mobilization were published in several journals.

West Point's mission is to produce "... leaders of character committed to the values of Duty, Honor, Country and prepared for a career of professional excellence and service to the nation ...." Joe Muckerman clearly deserves his "Well done." And West Point: "Well done."

—*Tim Cronon & Anne Muckerman*

Reflections of Dad
From his daughter, Martha Muckerman Rivkin
2011

We always had dinner together growing up. I couldn't wait for Dad to come home, unless, of course, I was in trouble with Mom. Dad sat at the head of the table and Mom at the other end. It was here that Dad would tell us, "We have orders to go to..." followed by the eternal moment of silence, followed by "Why?—we just got here!" followed by "Where are we going?"

It would usually be summertime. Movers came, goodbyes were said to friends, hopes were shared that we would remain lifelong pen pals, and off we went.

Many of our journeys involved car trips. Some were in boats or trains. The black station wagon was by far the most travel friendly and popular. All vehicles had to be house pet friendly, often included potty seats in the back, melting crayons, chirping parrots, barking dogs, sickness, and the well-traveled line, "Are we there yet?" Stops at Stuckey's were hard to come by as Dad would always say, "Ten more miles."

Once we arrived at our stop-over motel, the swimming pool was first, and for additional fun there were the "insert a quarter" vibrating beds. Great times for pillow fights! Dad got us up early, complete with military taps. Sometimes there might be a carnival in town.

Needless to say, we were able to see so much of our own United States, all of which Dad was so proud. The times were turbulent, too. I remember a ride to Kansas City for shopping when the radio blurted out that Marilyn Monroe had died. There was the Bay of Pigs, the deaths of John Kennedy, Martin Luther King, Jr., Robert Kennedy, and the Vietnam War. Our home life, led by Mom and Dad, was good and we survived and learned from these events.

Dad was always proud of us, and we knew it. We were proud of him too—in his Army uniform, standing tall, commanding his troops, loving his wife, our mother. Always there was a welcome heart, and a compassionate one. I will miss him forever, but feel, in some small way, I am part of his legacy.

Tribute to Col. (retired) Joseph E. Muckerman II
From his son, Edward C. Muckerman II
March, 2012

Dear Dad,

We made our peace years and years ago and as I look back, we had become the best of friends. When I first learned about the cancer that ultimately took you, it hurt so much that I felt as if someone had hit me in the stomach. Those last few weekends we had together were very special. I will always remember the drive we took to Rehoboth and to Bethany Beach, bringing back memories of the long bike rides that we used to take. Riding bikes in Lewes gave both of us the freedom to think and talk about life, but most importantly it gave us the best quality time one could imagine.

I will always remember your wisdom and logic for dealing with anything related to life, marriage, business, or the daily issues that were bothering us. You taught us all to do the right things at all times. That philosophy has helped me steer away from people with poor character and I am proud to say that I have lived that philosophy.

We are all taking care of Mom and I think that I have taken a leadership role in helping her through a lot of important decisions and financial planning problems. You did not have to tell me to do this, but I know what you expected from us. I think you would be very proud of Anne for what she has done to stay in Lewes and live independently.

I wish you could have been there to see John graduate from high school and to see Toni and me celebrate thirty years of marriage. I know that you lived a full life and you made your contribution to society every day. I am amazed by the number of friends you had. Mom has reached out to all of them and so many feel the way we all do, that you made a difference in all of our lives.

Growing up, we always knew that we would be moving every two to three years and whenever we moved it was always an adventure and an opportunity to meet new friends and see different places. To this day I don't know how you and Mom did it but our lives always seemed to be settled after a few months at a new base. We lived in some great cities and we had a lot of fun in every city we lived in. Key West is at the top of my list, followed by Ft. MacArthur in California, and Carlisle was a great place too. I have many memories of playing baseball in Carlisle and getting involved with Scouting. Mom played a big part in my scouting years but I cherish the memory of making it to Eagle Scout and having you there with me too to accept my last medal. That was the proudest day of my young life.

In later years we attended Minerallac meetings together and you taught me valuable lessons concerning the evaluation process during strategic decision making. How many Sunday walks did we take to talk about life, the world, and politics? Even when we did not agree, you always kept a positive approach to settling, or amicably accepting, differences of opinion. I so miss our daily conversations and I have missed my best friend.

I know that you did everything right in your life and I will carry that model with me the rest of my life. We had a great time growing up and you were always there to bail us out of our mistakes and messes, something that I will try to help my own children with. I can't fill your shoes but I will always try, and I will never forget that you were the best Dad that any of us could dream of.

Love always, Ed

Joseph E. Muckerman II

From his son, Peter Muckerman

2012

Finding the right place to start is quite tough, so let me begin by saying that I feel incredibly fortunate to have had my dad for a father. From my earliest memories it was always clear to me that his love for our family was paramount. He proved this repeatedly by his words and by his actions. It was always obvious that this love of family, and in general his respect for his fellow man, had been strongly rooted in his upbringing. Knowing my grandfather, whom I adored, it was clear where this love and respect originated.

As we grew up, my father always said that we should be what we wanted and do things that would make us happy in life. Dad was an optimist through and through—he could always find the positive in anything. I have always envied this and tried my best to emulate him.

I love the fact that Dad went to West Point and was born on the 4th of July—what a wonderful combination, so fitting to both the Academy and to such a great national holiday! I also adored his faith, especially during the time before his death. We could see that he was completely at peace with himself, knowing that this was the natural next step and that he was ready for the trip. He was not afraid. I have heard it said that people who are not afraid of death are those who have the greatest faith. By this measure alone, he probably felt on top of the world.

I am fortunate to have a multitude of wonderful and very much treasured memories, being blessed to have had such a great father. This particular one is a favorite. Many years ago when I was a teenager and just starting to spread my wings and stay out after dark, my father would always say, "Just be in by 11 o'clock." And I, of course, would say, "Sure." Being young, I believed that I was invincible and much smarter than my parents. To get to my own room I would first have to pass by my parents' door. I could manage this for the most part, but the difficulty was the creaky floor boards on the landing right outside of their bedroom. There were boards that I could step on without making a noise, but avoiding the ones that would announce a trespasser took the skill of a ballet dancer.

After years of believing that I had been successful in navigating these stairs and feeling very clever, one morning on the way to church Dad asked me when I had gotten in the night before. I hesitated, but ultimately spit out, "Well, around 11." My father quickly replied, "Try 12 o'clock and don't do it again." Of course I was petrified, but I never got in late again. Embarrassment dawned when I realized that I had not been as successful as I had thought in my efforts to gain a silent passage past my parents' room.

At Dad's funeral I felt honored to deliver the eulogy. I told the story that I had remembered from childhood when I asked my father if he would become a general. He answered that this probably would not happen because he had once taken the side of an officer who he felt had been wronged and that had angered Dad's own superior officer who was very influential with regard to future promotions. Dad knew what this would cost him but he remained true to what he believed. I think that while West Point is in the business of training soldiers and leaders, its primary mission is to train "Men and Women of Honor" and this is what my father was. He cared more about what was in his heart than what was on his shoulder.

In closing the eulogy I said that when a person dies, there are those who will say, "He is in a better place now." I would not dream of debating that, but I also believe that my father was in a good place here. How can someone be in a bad place when he is surrounded by love?

My Father, Joseph E. Muckerman II

By his daughter, Lucy Muckerman Lamb

May 2011

I adored my father. The sun rose and set upon his tall shoulders. The same ones that carried me home from the hospital, gave me strength and courage to face any obstacle, and later held his granddaughter Emily for the first time just minutes after she was born. His strong hand held on tight to Jocelyn as she took her first steps. His lap was the perfect resting spot for Caroline as she napped on a sunny afternoon in the back yard. His arms gave the perfect hugs for Landon and Hollis.

I was born in Key West, Florida, during my parents' assignment at the Naval Base there in 1966. Although Hurricane Inez was bearing down on the island at the time of my arrival, he was there by my mother's side as he always was. He proudly told the story that following my birth, he went home to tell my siblings that they had a new baby sister. Then, he promptly had them all go to church to celebrate this happy occasion. Our family moved on to Carlisle, Pennsylvania, and then to Fort MacArthur in San Pedro, California. I don't recall much from Carlisle, PA, since I was so young. My first recollection is our home on the base in California and my pet rabbit. Norbel was his name and he was all white. The rabbit scratched me all over as I tried to hold it and probably dress it up in doll clothes. To my dismay, Norbel went to a "farm" when we left for Virginia. Our California home on the Fort MacArthur base faced a large, round, grassy circle where a helicopter would occasionally land to take my father off to what seemed a very important meeting of some sort. He would take me for walks along the beach that was nearby. He always loved the salt air, sand, and water.

My most vivid memories are here in the Belle Haven home where my family now resides and where my parents lived for almost 35 years. I was five years old when we moved to this home from California. My father was a busy man but never too busy to spend time with me. One of my favorite memories is waiting at the end of the front steps for my father to return from work at the end of the day. He would pull up in his car and have the prize from the Cracker Jack popcorn box ready for me. I couldn't wait to tear it open to reveal the little trinket. Mom packed his lunch every day. I still wince when I think of the sardine sandwich that my mom would occasionally put in his lunch bag. Later, we would carpool back and forth from Belle Haven to his job at the Pentagon and my job at the White House. It was a 30-minute ride each way and an opportunity to talk and catch up on the day's events. One day we discovered we would both be at the same local hotel. He had a meeting and I was helping with a presidential in-town event. It turned out that he was able to chat and have a photo-op with President George H.W. Bush that day. There were many exciting days and events involving President Bush including a meet-and-greet at Belle Haven Country Club, Camp David departures from the South Lawn, tours of the West Wing, and shows viewed from the presidential box at the Kennedy Center.

One day on our way home from work in 1992, I told Dad that Sig Rogich had been nominated to be the US Ambassador to Iceland and that Sig had asked me to go along as his Executive Assistant at the U.S. Embassy. At that time, I couldn't imagine anything worse than leaving the safety of my sourroundings and routine and traveling thousands of miles away for an uncertain time period to a wintery, ice-cold foreign country. I didn't speak the Icelandic language nor would I know anyone else besides the U.S. Ambassador. Sure enough, Dad's words of wisdom carried over and he explained the grand opportunity being offered to me and the confidence to accept the unknown in this situation. Dad never doubted me and knew I would be just fine. So off to Baltimore-Washington International Airport with a one-way ticket in hand to Reykjavik, Iceland. Not to mention that I was newly engaged to Faron Lamb with a wedding planned for September 1992. The Iceland adventure turned out to be a short-term job opportunity. President Bush called Ambassador Rogich back to Washington, D.C., in September as a last ditch effort to help his campaign for reelection. I was back in the United States for my September wedding and returned to Iceland in October to pack my things. It was an invaluable experience to live overseas, experience embassy life and the Foreign Service, and know that anything was possible...one of the greatest gifts my father gave me.

My father's birthday was on the 4th of July. Every year we would have a family celebration to mark his birthday as well as the holiday. We would start early in the morning and had the ice cream maker churning before long. Homemade chocolate chip ice cream…it doesn't get much better than that. He commented that it was nice to always have a holiday on your birthday and that when he was a young boy, he thought the fireworks were for him.

Every holiday was a joyful and happy time here at our home in Belle Haven. If only the walls could talk; there would be many happy tales. The main reason that I wanted to move back to my childhood home is that it holds all these special memories inside. Now, with five daughters, we can continue the traditions and memories for years to come.

I recall the Thanksgiving holiday in November 2000. My father had been diagnosed with prostate cancer and was being treated with radiation-type medicine. I also happened to be pregnant with my fourth daughter, Landon, at the time. Somewhere in the literature or medical information packet for the radiation procedure there was a warning to avoid being in contact or near pregnant women during the course of the treatment. Well, we consulted with Dad's doctor and my obstetrician and they commented that this was the first time they had ever been posed with this question. I was not going to miss Thanksgiving dinner with Mom and Dad so we came up with a plan. Dad called his dentist, Dr. Ralph Jordan, and asked to borrow his protective bib that he used for patients when taking x-rays. Once again, this was the first time he had ever had this request. Surely you can picture us all sitting at the dining room table that Thanksgiving night with Dad at the head of the table in his dress pants, shirt and tie along with a large gray bib covering his torso from neck to belt area. If only we had a photo. This is a perfect example of the lengths that Dad would go to to make sure he could be with his grandkids.

I have a photo of Emily's fifth birthday party held at the local recreation center in February 1999. Dad had gone along to help out. A photo I will treasure is that of Grandpa painting Emily's fingernails with nail polish.

On the occasion of Landon's birth, Faron called my father and gave him the warning that he thought I was beginning labor. It had to have been around 4:00 am on April 20, 2001. Dutifully, Dad arrived at our home on Fort Hill Drive shortly thereafter to stay with Emily, Jocelyn, and Caroline while we went to the hospital. Well, in the course of those 15 minutes or so, things had gone from bad to worse and I was doubled over in excruciating pain. Dad was at a complete loss to see his daughter in such agony and immediately asked where our dog Goldie was. Thankfully, Faron and I made it to Alexandria Hospital in time and Landon was born about two minutes after we arrived at the hospital. Our favorite story was that Mom told Dad that he should eat some breakfast before he left for our house…thank goodness he didn't.

We went to the zoo, the park, lunch, picnics, or just for a walk. He always had time for me and my daughters. I always had time for him. He knew when I needed a break and would offer to watch the girls so Mom and I could go shopping or have lunch. We would usually return home to find Dad asleep on the sofa with one of the girls asleep by his side.

On my wedding day in September 1992, I got ready for the big day at the Belle Haven home. It was under renovation but that did not deter us from our plans. I chose to wear the dress that my mom wore on her wedding day. Once I was dressed and ready to go, I walked down the stairs and I will always remember the look on my father's face as he saw his youngest child now as a bride and in the dress that he surely remembered from his own wedding day in October 1953. We went by limousine to St. Mary's Church and as we prepared to walk down the aisle, you could see the tears in my father's eyes. They were tears of happiness. He knew that I had found a good man who truly loved me. He told me that the first time he met Faron at Brown's Volvo he knew there was something unique about him. They hit it off right away. Dad had a good sense about people and could see sincerity, honesty, and goodness.

It turns out that Dad gained a third son once Faron became part of the family and later five granddaughters. Faron immediately recognized the loving and caring nature of my father as well as his wisdom. There was nothing Faron enjoyed more than just spending time with Dad, whether it be winterizing the marina or going for a bike ride. Faron's father passed away when Faron was a young boy so he welcomed the opportunity to have a father in his life.

During my teenage years, Mom, Dad, and I would venture down to Washington, D.C., for the day on Saturday. We would go to the downtown Garfinckel's store and spend the day browsing among the many floors of fashionable outfits. Later we would have lunch at Old Ebbitt Grille or at a nearby restaurant. The Garfinckel's stores closed their doors long ago but the fond memories remain along with a few white boxes with the navy blue top and the gold lettering.

Dad's parents lived in Boulder, Colorado, during their retirement years. We would visit them each summer. Sometimes we would go to Estes Park, Steamboat Springs, or Long's Peak during our time in Colorado. E.C. and Joey were kind and loving grandparents and their influence was apparent in Dad's good nature. I can say with complete certainty that E.C. and Joey were so proud of Dad, his military career, his family, and the father that he had become. My father never once disappointed his parents.

I would take many, many pages to write about all of the wonderful memories that I cherish of my days and years with my father. But the most important message to relay is that I feel like the luckiest person in the world to have had Joe Muckerman as my father. I don't have a single regret about my 43 years with my father other than I wish he could have been with us longer. His love was unconditional and his wisdom unparalleled. He was a phenomenal man, father, grandfather, and friend to many. He will always be alive in my heart.

From his granddaughter, Emily Lamb

2010

Dear Greatest Grandpa in the World,

I miss you so much!

It was really hard not to cry when you left us. I was thinking, 'what if I had one wish?" I would wish that there was a cure for cancer. When Mom told me that you had stomach cancer and that the doctors couldn't do anything, my heart dropped and broke into a million pieces. I just kept thinking of anything the doctors could do to save you. I would give everything I have for you to come back.

I will never forget the day you gave me your necklace. It meant so much to me. Whenever I wear it I know that you are with me. I always looked up to you. . I will never forget you. You are gone but you will never be forgotten. I think about you every day. I couldn't have asked for a better grandpa.

On the 4th of July it was really sad because you weren't there to celebrate the day and your birthday. I was really disappointed because we left Delaware and got home late in the afternoon and I was really looking forward to celebrating with you and watching the fireworks.

I wish we could go for a bike ride together. Everyone always remembers you riding your bike around the "hood." I also wish that we could go to Pearl Harbor together. I hope to go there one day. It's hard going to Delaware and not seeing you there. I really miss your great hugs.

I remember when I was little and I was sad. I don't remember what I was sad about but you gave me a penny, I think it is from England. I still have it in my jewelry box. You always knew how to make someone feel better. Whenever we both looked at each other we would both just smile. You didn't have to say anything.

Say HI to E.C., Gram, Nancy, and Joey for me. I love you! This letter was written with love and hugs!

Love, Emily

Handwritten letter was placed in her grandfather's coffin.

From his granddaughter, Jocelyn Lamb

June 29, 2010

Dear Grandpa,

It has been a tough couple of weeks. I am going to Camp Seafarer tomorrow.

Don't worry, I still want to go to West Point and I promise you that I will do whatever it takes to get there. I just wish that you were still here to see me go. I know that it will make you really happy.

I have been taking care of everyone, especially Grandma. She is strong, and like you, she loves her family. She got so excited when I told her that hundreds of people would come to your funeral mass and there would only be standing room.

I went to Lewes last weekend with Emily, Uncle Peter, Grandma, and Nora. It was hard, and it wasn't the same without you. That was the worst 4th of July ever! I didn't celebrate too much, but I made sure that Carl raised your flag back up on your birthday.

There are many bad reasons that you died, like I will miss you. But, there are also good things that came out of it. I feel that the family has grown even closer. People are aspiring to be like you more. You had such a great life here. Now, we all need to let God take care of you. I'm sure you're having a big party up in Heaven with everyone. Everyone says that Joe Muckerman did not go through purgatory, but went straight to Heaven. Grandma really liked that when I told her.

So let's all raise a Bud-light glass to you for being faithful and honorable to everything and everyone, especially your family. I hope to be like you one day if I'm lucky. Make sure to say hi to everyone in Heaven, especially my Grandma Nancy. Tell her that Faron is the best Dad in the world.

Love, Jocelyn

Handwritten letter was placed in her grandfather's coffin.

From his granddaughter, Caroline Lamb

2010

Dear Grandpa,

I love you so much. I miss you a lot too. Even though I can't see you, you're still here with me. We are all still very sad but we know you're watching out for us. I didn't want you to leave us, but I didn't want you to suffer. We're taking care of Grandma. She's doing a lot better now. Camp was so fun and so was Lewes Night Out. I remember you always loved it. Thanks for being in my life. I love you.

Love, Caroline

Handwritten letter was placed in her grandfather's coffin.

From his granddaughter, Landon Lamb

2010

Dear Grandpa,

I miss you so much. At the mass I was about to cry but I cried at church. You went to Heaven right write (sic) after you died. I was sad at camp cause you died. I wanted to write to you. I think about you all the time. You are the best grandpa ever. I will keep praying for you. I love you so much.

Love, Landon

Handwritten letter was placed in her grandfather's coffin.

From his granddaughter, Hollis Lamb

2012

Although Hollis was only six years old at the time of her grandfather's passing in 2010, she had grown to love and adore him as if she had known him for many more years.

Grandpa Joe would always bring Hollis lollipops from his visits to the bank. We stopped by the Lewes branch one time and the bank tellers said, "You must be Mr. Muckerman's granddaughters." After his death, Hollis looked remorseful and said, "Now who is going to bring us lollipops?"

Later, at family dinner, we had roasted a turkey and Hollis was insistent on getting the wishbone. Holding the wishbone as she thought carefully, she told me that she really, really wanted a hot tub but her wish was for Grandpa to come back alive.

The school bus stop is about a block from our house. Recently, as we walked toward the bus stop in the early morning, the sun rays were coming through the trees and casting a beautiful glow on the street. Hollis exclaimed as she looked at the sight, "Look, it is Grandpa shining down on us from Heaven."

I asked Hollis for her thoughts on Grandpa and she wrote, "I love Grandpa be cuz he loves me!"

Only from a child's point of view can come such simple and beautiful words following the death of a loved one.

reported by her mother, Lucy Muckerman Lamb

From his grandson, Christian Muckerman

November 10, 2010

Dear Grandpa,

I am writing you this letter although you will never read it. I think about you so often and the things I wish I said to you before you passed. Although you are gone there is something that makes me feel like you are still here. With your death, I learned more about you. You were not just my grandfather, but a Colonel in the United States Army. I have learned more about what that meant after you died than when you were alive.

The day you passed I was away at camp. When the counselors came to pick me up to bring me to the office where my brother and I were going to get the call from my Dad, my brother asked me, "Why do you think they brought us here?" I told him that I didn't know, but in my mind I knew we were going to get the call that said you had died. I had so many questions for Mom and Dad, but at that moment I couldn't really think of the words to ask, or even exactly what I wanted to ask.

So much time passed between the time that you died and when we finally got to Arlington for your burial. Even though we had the funeral at the church back in June, it never seemed like we got to say goodbye until we had the service at the National Cemetery at Arlington, with so many special things that described your life. I don't think that I really understood your life in the military until I saw the horses with the caisson, the band, the trumpeter, and the rigid soldiers that folded the flag that they gave to Grandma. It wasn't just that everything was so impressive, so much as the feeling that I got when I saw all of the people who came to see you off, and how important you were to all of the soldiers. We were the most important people in the cemetery because we were your family. I finally understood what it meant to be in the Army.

Having our family – your sister's family – all gathering together and remembering you, but also celebrating your life was also something special that I will always remember. You meant so much to so many people, but also you brought so many people together. Even though I miss you, I feel so special that I am part of your family and that you are part of mine.

They gave us some of the shells from your twenty-one gun salute. The metal casings remind me of the wars you were in, but they don't really remind me of you. I am impressed by your military service, but you were more important than that to me. You were my Grandpa Joe.

Love, your grandson, Christian

p.s. I wish you were still with us.

Colonel Joseph Edward Muckerman II

From his granddaughter, Jocelyn Lamb

2010

Lewes, Delaware, is one of my favorite places in the whole world. It is a comforting place. It used to feel like nothing could ever go wrong there. I felt safe and my friends and family always surrounded me. I could go to estate sales with my grandparents, walk on the beach or ride my bike with my dad. My dad is a person everyone loves, and my grandpa was, too.

I was camping in the mountains when I found out that my grandfather had stomach cancer. It would be a couple of weeks before I could get to Lewes to visit him. When I saw him, I immediately noticed the difference in how he looked. That feeling that I had before, that Lewes was perfect, disappeared in an instant. I didn't know if I would ever get it back. I wanted everything to go back to normal, but life as I knew it would soon be changing.

We travelled back to Lewes every chance we could before school ended. I would have walked miles just to see him. So many people loved my grandfather. I never met anyone who didn't. He changed people's lives with a kind word or a simple act of kindness. If you were in the room with him, you would be the sole focus of his attention and he would listen to every word you had to say. He made everyone feel special. My mother told me many stories from when she was growing up. My grandfather was one of a kind. You could say that with confidence. Wherever he went, he left his mark—overseas, in my neighborhood, and in my heart.

My dad loved my grandfather. He told me that Grandpa was his best friend. They loved riding bikes or working on the marina. My dad didn't know his own father. He was raised by his mother and grandmother after his father passed away at a young age. Grandpa treated my dad like his own son. On Father's Day just a short time before his death, Grandpa pulled my Dad aside and gave him his West Point class ring. He wanted my father to have it until the day he could pass it on to me at West Point. He said, "I love you, Son." With tears in his eyes, my father said, "I love you too, Dad." As it turned out, my dad did have a father after all.

One evening in June, we all went down to the marina, like old times. There was a nice cool breeze that kept the bugs away, which was rare. It was such a nice night. The sun started to set, turning the sky an array of different shades of orange. We didn't have to say anything. Listening to the faint sound of crickets, we sat there and saluted the boats that passed by. There was no place in the world that I would have rather been.

Later I sat with Grandpa in the house for a while and we talked. He asked me about my hopes for college. I told him I wanted to attend West Point. It took some effort, but he gave me the biggest smile that reached both of his ears and said, "You would be perfect."

That was the last time I would ever talk with him and the last time I would see those big blue eyes of his. The next day he was unresponsive. I still talked to him though, because they say that a person can still hear you when near death. I tried so hard to talk, but my throat burned and felt as if it was closing up. I managed to get a few sentences out.

My grandmother is very strong like my grandpa but she couldn't say a word, and I don't blame her for it. I said something to him for her. They loved each other so deeply after fifty-six years of married life.

He passed away without any pain but everyone was crying. I think I had an endless blank expression full of sadness on my face but I held his hand and said a prayer. I thought to myself, "If he can't make it to Heaven, then no one can." I took one last look at him and kissed him on his forehead.

June 26, 2010, was my grandfather's final salute. I will remember my grandfather as a hero, a soldier fighting his last battle. Death may have won that battle, but my grandfather won the war. That, I can be sure of. My grandfather never gave up, even when they said there was no hope. He lived his life to the fullest, to the very last second. That is how I want to live and be remembered too. He was faithful and honorable to everything and everyone he cared about, especially our family.

Eulogy from the Memorial Mass on August 9, 2010

St. Jude's Catholic Church, Lewes, Delaware

Given by Ted Becker, Friend and City Council Member

I met Joe and Anne nearly 20 years ago as we were all becoming part of the community of Lewes. Our friendship has always been Lewes based, but over the years our frequent discussions have provided a much more broad-based perspective of Joe's life beyond the limits of this community.

It came as no surprise to me that Joe was a native of St. Louis, Missouri, also my native city and state. As you may know, Missouri enjoys the nickname of being the "Show Me State." I believe it can be said that Joe was always true to Missouri's nickname as he was firm in his opinions and beliefs while open to possibility of change and was always dedicated to the "Common Sense" approach to challenges of life.

While Joe loved living in their homes in Alexandria and Third Street here in Lewes, it was their move to the Pilottown Road house that provided him a true sense of being a Lewes resident. He would frequently discuss how he looked forward to their weekly trip to Lewes and hoped to convince Anne to "give up" Alexandria and make Lewes their full-time home. While this actually occurred this past February, in the middle of one of our worst winters, Joe had long before developed many habits and characteristics that made him part of the fiber of this community.

His participation in the many philanthropic events of this community is one way of his involvement, but his early Saturday morning bike rides, rain or shine, to scout the local yard sales for undiscovered treasures, his mowing the lawn in the middle of a hot day, or his regular Saturday lunch of a "Power House Sandwich" at the Second Street Grille also represented his level of integration into this community.

While many might be content having found this level of personal satisfaction, Joe always saw a bigger picture. He had a keen interest in political matters, national security issues, and developmental progress. I am sure these interests were in part a result of his military education and service. It was those interests and his pursuit of information that led him to write letters to the editors of various newspapers and politicians sharing his thoughts and opinions. Always well thought out and to the point, Joe was proud to take a position and explain his rationale for the same. In fact, my last conversation with him was largely focused on a letter he had written to the *Washington Post*. It was published just days after his passing.

While Joe pursued all of these community and national endeavors and interests, he found his greatest pleasure in his relationship with Anne, his children, and grandchildren. Whether it was a holiday get-together, a getaway to celebrate a special family occasion, or a weekend visit here in Lewes, Joe was proud of his family and their achievements. He often would share stories of their accomplishments and was always looking forward to the next event.

Together with Anne, he built their antiques business from a small part-time hobby into a successful venture that provided both fun and focus and hopefully some profit. Acting as sounding boards for one another over which items to buy, they would gather their various finds, each providing for the other's overindulgence. It was always a pleasure to watch them display merchandise and hear the stories that happened along the way. Joe was the practical one wondering if something would "fit" in the car or in the space, but Anne found a way to bring it together. I feel certain their approach to the antiques business was a direct reflection of the life they had built together–one of love and respect with opportunity for each to grow.

I believe Joe's sense of family and his continued interest and devotion to his beliefs gave him a fullness of life that is not often achieved.

And it made him a person that we are all better for having known.

Tribute to Joseph E. Muckerman, II

From Col. (ret.) David Garner

2012

Joe Muckerman was the consummate Christian gentleman. In every situation I ever observed Joe, he was considerate, patient, understanding, and one who sought to bring out the best in everyone and to bring "light, not heat" to every endeavor. His low-key (but very effective) approach contrasted with his passionate determination to improve our nation's security and preparedness.

I first met Joe in 1985, when he was the Director of Emergency Preparedness on the Under Secretary of Defense for Policy staff and I headed the Mobilization Plans branch on the Joint Staff. Because of our intersecting areas of interest, we worked closely together for the next three years. We participated together in several mobilization exercises, worked closely with the Federal Emergency Management Agency (FEMA), had special relationships with his colleagues in the Office of the Secretary of Defense (OSD) dealing with industrial preparedness and mobilization, and shared mutual interests and involvement in the Global War Games conducted at the Naval War College and our special relationship with Canada.

During the years 1985-1988, we were in the last throes of the Cold War—only we didn't know that at the time!—and still planning for the possibility of a major war with the Soviet Union over the Warsaw Pact. Joe was in the forefront of ensuring that the Department of Defense and the nation's industrial base were adequately prepared for that eventuality, and worried that maybe our nation wasn't as prepared as it should have been.

During my years on the Joint Staff there was great mistrust between the Organization of the Joint Chiefs, as they were then known, and the Office of the Secretary of Defense staff, primarily because OSD leadership were political appointees. However, Joe and I quickly bonded; there was never a question of "trust" between Joe and me and that was because of Joe's honesty. It was clear to me from the start that Joe was someone I could trust, and I hoped he harbored similar feelings towards me.

We could be in contentious meetings together, but Joe was unflappable; his quiet demeanor reflected a steadfastness of character that was evident to all with whom he interacted.

We shared podiums, as at the Army War College, and shared ideas. Joe was a true patriot! We shared a background as artillery officers, Joe in the Army and me in the Marine Corps. As it turned out, we shared religion, too, as we were both Catholic. And we shared the same outlook, which he certainly fostered in me, that there was only one special interest in our work and that was the "national interest."

Joe was always open to ideas on how we could mutually do our jobs better. When I was a neophyte to Emergency Preparedness and Mobilization, I often sought his counsel. We participated in venues with some of the veterans who mobilized industry and the country during World War II. During my tenure on the Joint Staff, Joe mentored me, with me being only somewhat aware at that time of how effective he had been. He supported our successful effort on the Joint Staff to increase the President's authority to activate Reserves, which greatly benefited our nation in the run-up to Desert Storm.

We maintained our professional relationship after I left the Joint Staff and retired from the Marine Corps. Working for the Logistics Management Institute (LMI), our paths continued to cross at the Global War Games and OSD-sponsored mobilization exercises. For OSD's Proud Eagle exercise, LMI had been awarded the task to evaluate the Department's effectiveness for the Under Secretary for Policy, with Joe as the Task Monitor. His guidance was simple—"observe the exercise from 20,000 feet." He wasn't interested in detailed machinations, but rather, the view from an over-arching perspective.

A team of us evaluated key portions of the exercise and I ended up briefing our results to OSD senior management, creating somewhat of a firestorm with the recently established U.S. Transportation Command (TRANSCOM). LMI had evaluators at the TRANSCOM components, but not at TRANSCOM Headquarters. Our perspective on coordination among the components was less generous than TRANSCOM leadership believed, so, I was called to brief TRANSCOM senior leadership. Joe went with me to TRANSCOM Headquarters, supported our findings, and "had my back."

After Joe retired, we remained in contact, still interested in ensuring the preparedness of the United States. The geo-strategic world had changed drastically, but our relationship and friendship remained constant. I was honored to be a friend of Joe's. Joe was a paragon in the emergency preparedness community, who often sought his advice and counsel. Most importantly, Joe was a quiet, confident counselor who was greatly respected and admired by all with whom he came in contact. The nation owes Joe Muckerman a debt of gratitude for his contributions to our security. He faithfully served his God, his nation, and his family—he was quite a man!

End Notes

Foreword

1. After completion of military service that included combat service during WWII and assignment as an Army platoon leader in Korea, John Patrick McBride was led to join the Jesuits in 1952 and ordained a Priest in the Society of Jesus on June 17, 1961. He worked for 20 years in a maximum security federal prison, followed by 15 years at Providence Portland Medical Center. He retired in June,1971 and is currently living in Spokane, Washington.

The importance of Father John's personal friendship and spiritual guidance to Joe and to Anne is immeasurable. To this book he added the Foreword and the title.

Chapter One – An American Boyhood

"Pa Joe's Story," drafted notes written by Joseph E. Muckerman II, provide all of the firsthand accounts and family history for these pages, except where noted. Joseph E. Muckerman II drafted notes appear in their entirety in the Appendix.

1. City of St. Louis, Missouri – certified copy of birth certificate states that Joseph Edward Muckerman II was born at Barnes Hospital on July 4, 1926 to Edward Christopher Muckerman, age 25, whose profession is stated as "Mgr." and Josephine Schmieder Muckerman, age 23, "Housewife," both residing at 7136 Forsythe. The live birth was certified by the attending physician, R. Crossen and registered on July 9, 1926.

2. "The Muckermans – The Christopher & Wilhelmina Branch," a family history compiled by Chris J. Muckerman in 1972. Unpublished.

3. From "A History of St. Louis" (www.st.louis.org): The Great Depression hit St. Louis harder than many areas. When 15.9 percent of all Americans were out of work in 1931, almost one in four St. Louisans were unemployed. Local manufacturing production declined more than the national average during the Depression, and

never felt the slight recovery precipitated by the National Recovery Administration in 1935. Some industries never recovered.

4. From *St. Louis Commerce* Magazine – May/June 2009, issue No. 3. When war began in Europe in 1939, Chamber of Commerce President Thomas N. Dysart thought St. Louis should prepare – in case the U. S. became involved. This resulted in a comprehensive census of area manufacturers, facilities and labor statistics. Copies were sent to each of the 1100 prime defense contractors in the nation. St. Louis had at least a six-month start on other cities when the U. S. began shipping armaments and supplies to Europe. By the end of WWII, at least 420 St. Louis area plants worked on direct defense contracts. The St. Louis Chamber of Commerce became a full time war agency and supported every patriotic project from Bundles for Britain to collecting aluminum for scrap drives.

5. Real estate records document that 44 Crestwood Drive_was built in 1935.

6. Letter from Wally Schmieder to Anne Muckerman.

7. "The Muckermans – The Christopher & Wilhelmina Branch", a family history compiled by Chris J. Muckerman in 1972. Unpublished.

8. *St Louis Commerce* Magazine, Issue No. 3, May/June, 2009.

9. "Joe wanted to join the Army." Conversation between Timothy Cronin and Wally Schmieder in 2011.

10. "St. Louis Downtown Airport History," www. stlouisdowntownairport.com, re: Oliver Parks.

From 1939 – 1944 Oliver Parks operated Parks Air College whose facilities expanded to several mid-western locations. By the end of World War II, fully one-sixth of all U. S. Army Air Corps pilots of the era were trained at Parks' Midwestern Facilities.

11. "The Life and Times of Oliver Parks," *Universitas*, the Magazine of St. Louis University, Vol. 7/No. 1, Summer, 1981.

After a near fatal airplane crash, Oliver Parks converted to Catholicism and entered into a close relationship with the Jesuit community in St. Louis. Ultimately Parks would donate the land of his first flying school to help establish St. Louis University, requiring him to move Parks Air College directly across the river to East St. Louis, Illinois. Parks remained devoted to the Jesuits and to the university all of his life.

12. Possibly as a result of the changing geography of the Parks Air College and the required number of candidates to the Military Academy per state, E. C. Muckerman and Joe established residency at Parks Flying School, East St. Louis, Illinois, and his appointment came through the State of Illinois.

11. "The Millard School and Millard Foundation" by Bill Marvel, www.brandonhistoricalmuseum.org.

12. First letter from West Point to home, dated July 9, 1945: "I don't mind it here, it is not like Millard's – you never get enough time to think about your troubles."

Chapter Two – Duty, Honor, Country

1. Letter from Edward Muckerman to Joe, July 2, 1945. Entire text in Appendix.

2. and 3. Collected letters from Joseph E. Muckerman II to his family.

4. Timothy Cronin, West Point classmate, writing Joe's tribute for TAPS, a supplement to July-September *ASSEMBLY*, the West Point magazine.

5. Timothy Cronin, letter of May 16, 2011.

6. Collected letters from Joseph E. Muckerman II to his family.

7. Timothy Cronin, TAPS.

8. Class statistics provided by M. G. (ret.) Lee Surut.

9. "Pa Joe's Story," Joseph E. Muckerman II draft. See Appendix.

10. Collected letters from Joseph E. Muckerman II to his family.

11, 12, 13. Timothy Cronin, letter of May 16, 2011.

14. Timothy Cronin, letter of July 22, 2011.

15. The U.S. Air Force was established as a separate service when President Harry Truman signed the National Security Act of 1947 in September of that year. Previous to this, the Army Air Corps was a branch of the U.S. Army.

16. Timothy Cronin, letter of July 22, 2011.

Chapter Three – La Vie en Rose

Memories recorded in this chapter are from Anne Muckerman's written notes, September 2010 and conversations between Anne Muckerman and Anne Hanzel over various meetings in 2010 and 2011.

Anne Butler Muckerman is the first of four daughters born to Martha Mary Ferguson and Henry Jocelyn Butler. Her childhood in Upper Ladue (St. Louis, Missouri) is remembered in the book, "Upper Ladue Remembers" by Anne Butler Muckerman and Beatrice Butler Toberman, 2008 by Acacia Publishing.

1. Villa Duchesne was founded in 1929, offering Catholic education to young women in grades 1 – 12 in the Sacred Heart tradition. The 60 acre campus in Frontenac is located at 801 South Spoede Road, St. Louis, MO. www.vdoh.org.

2.Anne Butler letters to Odile Stewert. In 2007 Anne Muckerman received a surprise packet of letters that she had written to her friend Odile Stewart Mecker during a period beginning in 1946 and ending in 1954 when Anne was a young wife and mother living in Ft. Sills and in Washington.

3. Truman Inauguration information from the website of the Truman Library, www.trumanlibrary.org.

4. The Iron Gate Restaurant was closed in 2010 but remains at 1734 North Street, NW, Washington, D.C. It was reviewed as one of the most romantic locations in Washington.

5. In 2000, the Department of Defense released revised figures for the official count of battle deaths for United States service members in Korea for the period 1950 – 1953. The DoD figure is 33,686. The previous and widely quoted number of 56,246 included deaths of all service members worldwide for this period and was identified as a clerical error. www.Defense.gov – "Korean War Dead Stats", June 8, 2000.

6. Twenty-nine members of the West Point Class of 1949 died in Korea. Information provided by M. G. (ret.) Lee Surut.

7. Martha Mary "Sissy" Butler married Nicholas von Guggenberg, July 8, 1950 and "Bede" Beatrice Cecilia Butler married Joseph Thomas Toberman on February 6, 1952. Anne Muckerman recalls that her sister Bede's wedding had to be arranged hurriedly because of the groom's service orders. The bridesmaids' dresses were purchased from the department store Famous-Barr and were subsequently purchased back by the store to accommodate another wedding party similarly under the time constraints imposed by the U. S. Military.

8. Brad Terry letter to Joe Muckerman, original in Anne Muckerman's personal papers.

9. Martha Butler was an accomplished artist whose paintings are in the possession of her family and grandchildren.

10. Later in their lives, Henry Butler and Martha Butler were able to re-establish a friendship.

11. The wedding and the honeymoon had to conform to Joe's orders to report to duty

at Ft. Riley, Kansas.

Mileage www.randmcnally.com:

St. Louis to Colorado Springs - 835 miles, Colorado Springs to Ft. Riley - 595 miles.

Chapter Four – The Army Life's For Me

1. General MacArthur was "fired" by President Harry Truman and removed from command in April 1951.

2. Performance Data: Letter of August 29, 1953 from Col. H. B. Hudiburg, Commanding Officer, 138th Antiaircraft Artillery Group. APO 994.

3. Performance Data: Officer Efficiency Report, May 18, 1954 - August 17, 1954.

4. Performance Data: Letter of Commendation signed by B. G. Thomas Watlington.

5. history.nasa.gov/sputnik.

6. Telephone conversation: Barney Broughton with Anne Muckerman.

7. Performance Data: Letter of Appreciation signed by Col. H. B. Ayers, Chief of the Army Staff Communications Office, August 6, 1956.

8. Full text in the Appendix.

9. Performance Data: Officer Efficiency Report, June 12, 1960 - September 26, 1960.

10. ibid, April 1, 1960 - June 22, 1960.

11. Letter from Joe Cunningham to Anne Muckerman.

12. usacac.army.mil, "About the Command and General Staff College."

13. Performance Data: Officer Efficiency Report, April 1, 1963 - March 31, 1964.

14. Performance Data: Officer Efficiency Report, March 13, 1965 - September 1, 1965.

15. ibid, October 29, 1964 - March 12, 1965.

16. Performance Data: Officer Efficiency Report, September 5, 1965 - September 4,

1966.

17. The *Key West Citizen*, August 4, 1966.

18. www.casamarinaresort.com/about-casa-marina/Resort-History.

19. Performance Data: Officer Efficiency Report, August 6, 1967 – June 10, 1968.

20. Letter from Howard Jelinek to Anne Muckerman and telephone conversation of June, 2012.

21. Performance Data: Officer Efficiency Report, June 11, 1969 – June 10, 1069.

22. "The Army's Forgotten Men" by Bob Embry.

23. "Four Batteries Survive Wild Brush Fire," by Irma Rogers, ARGUS, December, 1970.

24. ibid.

25. Performance Data: Officer Efficiency Report, November 7, 1951 - May 8, 1952.

26. "Bay of Pigs Revisited," by Col. Joseph E. Muckerman, *Military Review*, April, 1971. The announcement of the Military Review Article Award was made in the June, 1971 issue.

27. Performance Data: Officer Efficiency Report, period ending July, 1975.

28. ibid.

29. www.ndu.edu/icaf/about.

30. www.ndu.edu/icaf/about/enrollment.

31. Performance Data: Officer Efficiency Report, comments from Col. Laurence E. Randall dated July 8, 1976 and comments from M. G. Theodore Antonelli, dated July 23, 1976.

Chapter Five – Still Serving

1. www.defense.gov "Caspar W. Weinberger."

2, 3, 4. Col (ret) John Brinkerhoff, letter to Anne Muckerman, October 2012.

5. *Assignment Pentagon, the Insider's Guide to the Potomac Puzzle Palace,* by M. G.

Perry M. Smith, published 1993 by AUSA Books, page 206 - 207.

Chapter Six – Little House by the Bay

1. www.heritagefoundation.org

2. FEMA memo dated 8-28-2007 from R. David Paulson

3. Col. (ret.) John Brinkerhoff, letter to Anne Muckerman, October, 2012.

4. Alfred Duff Gordon, 1st Viscount Norwich, to his wife, Diana. Poem appeared in Cooper's 1953 autobiography, *Old Men Forget,* recounting his life in politics and his service to his native England during World War I. Duff Gordon died in 1954. Joe may have uncovered this book because Duff Gordon was a contemporary of Joe's own personal hero, Winston Churchill.

5. See Appendix - Larry C. Johnson, "The Declining Terrorist Threat," Opinion published in *The New York Times*, 7-10-2001 and letter from J. E. Muckerman, II in response, published in *The New York Times*.

Chapter Seven – Who Could Ask for Anything More?

In Joe's notes for his memoirs, included in Appendix, he dedicated his story to his family and added, "Who could ask for anything more?" That line was used in two popular published songs with lyrics by George Gershwin: "I've Got Rhythm" and "Nice Work If You Can Get It." Both refer to the idea of making one's own happiness, finding love, and remaining satisfied with that happiness.

1. *The New York Times*, 1-25-2004.

2. website of Association of the Miraculous Medal, 1811 W. St. Joseph Street, Perryville, Missouri.

3. *U. S. Military Criticized for Purchase of Russian Copters for Afghan Air Corps*, by Craig Whitlock, the Washington Post, 6-19-2010. See Appendix.

4. More than 800 voluntary members of the U.S. Armed Services who were killed in Afghanistan and Iraq are interred in Section 60.

Appendices

Letter from Edward Muckerman to his son, Joe Written from the Hotel Pierre, New York, July 2, 1945 and posted with a 3-cent stamp

Dear Joe,

It's a little after ten and I just returned from an eventful day at the Point. Certainly it is one I shall always remember for I witnessed the culmination of much effort and any anxious days on the part of both of us.

Until you have a son someday who I hope you can be as proud of as I was of you as you entered West Point you will never know exactly how I felt. I will describe my day. You will probably never be able to describe yours.

A U. S, Army Corporal who has nothing to do with the course at the Point but is stationed here on M.P. duty saw that I got a pass in. I believe I saw everyone there running around but you. What a work-out. While visiting Grant Hall I head the orders being barked out a mile a minute. They seemed to come so fast one might have trouble getting it all heard and done. No doubt you bit the old tongue more than once.

I met the parents of several of the boys who were there like I was. The boys are E. Craig Betts and Gerrit Van Westenbrugge. Maybe you know them.

Incidentally you looked like a veteran with a couple of them calling you "Muck." How many Millard's boys made it?

This I think is interesting. Mr. Betts had a son graduate in 1942, and has lived through and knows the facts. Some of them are these:

Beast Camp lasts 6 weeks and is tough. Some will drop out at the end of it. After a week or so of Beast Camp when the 2nd year men return, one or more can extend a hand which means when with them you are at ease in their rooms, etc.

If you have a voice you might make the choir, all are tried out. Do your best. Competition is keen – sing out.

You may ask for a watch in September and usually are allowed to wear them in October.

Christmas week is run on a schedule for the Cadet's amusement – the best orchestras from New York, much visiting by parents and a general good time.

The first year however is not too good, the rest not too difficult and many privileges and fun.

Pick your room mate wisely no change can be made after a selection.

All boodle must be consumed each night so don't send too much rather more often.

Football games swell.

I learned this, made a visit in the chapel, met Msgr. Murdock briefly. Cadets, when you get going, are always welcome at his spacious home on Saturday afternoons and Sundays. No Upper Classmen allowed. A real relax. You will like him I know.

I witnessed the induction in North Gym. Was one of the approximate hundred in the balcony. Was certain I saw you 4th row from the front right on the end. Do let me know if I was correct. You all looked great and did very well.

I imagine you were about as tired as after Long Peak climb when you hit the bed tonight. You will toughen up fast.

The worst day is over. B-Camp will pass don't let it throw you, remember Fr. Healy's words about testing real metal with fire.

I got soaked coming home and had dinner at Childs. Roast duck – good.

Our two days in New York were wonderful. I shall always remember them as among the happiest I spent. I surely hated to have to leave you there but better there than waving to you on a boat bound for the Far East.

You are a real Pal. New York is not the same without you but there will be other visits together.

Will enjoy a nights rest in a cool room.

Remember that Hail Mary once in a while and write if you need anything. Oh yes, did you need your letter of acceptance?

Am quite tired but thrilled enough over you to get this off tonight.

Love, Dad

Direct transcription of Joe Muckerman's memories, as written by him.

PA JOE'S STORY

Dedicated to my wife Anne, the love of my life, and to my children and their spouses and their children –

Who could ask for anything more?

PREFACE

I am writing this for two reasons:

1. I have had a very wonderful and interesting life and I believe that I have learned a lot, made some mistakes, but overall, I would like to pass on some history to those I love.
2. I really knew only one of my grandparents, Annie Schmieder. Grandfather Schmieder died before I was born and Dad's mother died in childbirth. I knew my namesake, Joe Muckerman I, but not well because he died when I was 10. My step-grandmother did not get along well with my Dad so we had very little contact with her after my grandfather's death. In sum, I want you all (grandchildren) to know Pa Joe!

Let me begin by relating what I do know about my grandparents and what has been passed down to me.

Grandfather Schmieder (1871-1919)

Franz Josef, Jr. was born in the village of Kleinflufenbarg in the Austrian Alps on 13, September, 1871 at 3 o'clock in the morning. His father, Franz Josef, ran a mill powered by steam which processed grain for farmers. When the Kaiser placed a surtax on each bag of grain that he proceeded, he refused to pay and was warned that he would be arrested. To avoid jail time, he packed up his wife and four children and escaped to Switzerland. From there he obtained United States immigration papers. (Franz Josef, Jr. was 12 at the time.)

The Schmieders settled in St. Louis where they had friends in the bakery business. Grandfather got a job delivering baked goods. At age 15 he became an apprentice baker and eventually saved enough money to buy the French Bakery located at Sarah and Cook Streets.

He married my grandmother, Anne Springmeyer, and the two of them ran a very successful business – he handling the wholesale part to hotels and railroads (26 horse drawn delivery wagons – he knew each horse by name) and Grandmother ran the over-the-counter business. Together, they expanded the business by installing electric dough mixers and adding to their delivery capacity.

All went well until the Union stepped in and tried to sabotage the business by putting lead bullets in the bread. Also, they had two drivers who delivered to saloons and would get drunk. In one instance a driver fell asleep on his way back to the bakery, but the horse knew the way and brought the still sleeping driver back to the stable.

Grandfather died in 1919 (age 48) after a long illness. (I asked my grandmother what caused his death and she answered "complications" "yellow jaundice".) Before his death, grandfather sold the bakery to Natziger Bakery for a nice sum.

He left his wife Anne Schmieder (with) a daughter, Josephine, age 17, and two sons, Francis, Jr. (Bud), age 10, and Walter (Wally), age 7.

Grandmother Schmieder (Annie/"Gram") was left a young widow (age 42) with a teenage daughter and two young sons. From what I can gather, she was devastated by her loss but carried on and raised three wonderful children.

Gram was one of the finest persons I have ever known. After her children were married or on their own, she adopted two teenage girls, Dorthy and Florence. I am not certain why these adoptions occurred but I do know that they (especially Dorthy) caused her some grief.

Eventually, after losing much of her inheritance during the Depression, she moved into our home and became a second mother. Dad adored her as did Mary Ann and I. During the summer we took the streetcar to the cemetery where her husband (our grandfather) was buried. We cut the grass around his horizontal tombstone and then we had a picnic lunch.

She never bawled us out when we were bad, but explained why we were wrong and gave us jobs around the house to keep us out of mischief. Gram did all of the cooking and helped my mother in a thousand different ways.

When we had a cottage in Douglas, Michigan, we (Mary Ann, Gram and I) would take the train there shortly after school ended. Upon arrival we worked to clean up the cottage and grounds in anticipation of our parents arrival in July.

One trait that I inherited from Gram was talking to strangers. Mom would often say when Gram retuned from church or shopping, "What took you so long?" "Well I met 'so and so' and we had a nice conversation." "But you didn't know (him/her/them)." "Well, I do now."

In her last years Gram had a stroke and was told she could never walk again. While home on leave from the Army, I went to her room and found her crawling on the floor. "Gram, what are you doing?!" "I am getting ready to walk again." And sure enough, she did.

What a great woman!

Joseph E. Muckerman, I

My namesake and Ned's.

As I mentioned earlier, Joe I died when I was 10. Thus, I do not have too many memories of him. But even with the relatively few contacts, I did have with my grandfather, I knew instinctively that he was a very bright and fine individual. I remember that he liked to play horse shoes and tennis. He also put sugar on tomatoes.

But now for a brief history of the Muckermans. *This section was never completed.*

Mom, Dad, and sister Mary Ann

I had a great family – two mothers, Gram and Josephine, and Edward – Joey, or Joe, and EC.

Since everyone called Mom, "Joe," I was renamed "Sonny," much to my dislike.

Dad's half sister Mary married Mom's brother Bud. Thus, we had double cousins.

The Schmieders lived down the street on Crestwood Drive in Clayton, Missouri.

Wally, my other uncle, is about 11 years older than I am and he was my first baby sitter. We have been very close ever since.

Dad's only full sister, Clara, married Bob Miller. They also lived nearby and had four children.

Family relationships among Dad's brothers and sisters, Mary (Schmieder) and Clara (Miller), Joe and John were strained due to the fact that Dad was co-executor of Joe I's estate (with my step-grandmother) and received a great deal of heat and misery from his step-mother and brothers and sisters. I do not know the details but on many occasions I asked, "What's wrong Dad?" "The estate distribution. I kicked the covers all night." John, Joe and Clara all got divorced and needed money. Mary and Bud moved to Arizona where all died, apparently from asbestos poisoning.

Joe I headed an ice and fuel company, Polar Ware and then, City Ice and Fuel. This was a family company and had five other Muckermans working there – Frank, Chris, Walter, John, and my Dad. I do not know the details but Dad was eased out and went to work at the Manchester Bank as Vice President. In sum, Dad got a lot of misery from his relations but he rose above it and was a great father and husband.

Much of his kindness and love for his family stemmed from the fact that he never knew his mother who died in childbirth. Thus, he spent his early years in the care of relatives (the Sanders). They took good care of him but he lacked the love only real parents can give. Because of this experience, Dad went out of his way to give Mary Anne and I a lot of attention and love.

I don't think he and Mom spoiled us – we always cleaned our plates, did our homework, cut the grass, polished our shoes and made our beds, etc.

In sum, I was blessed with the greatest Mom and Dad the Lord ever created.

One last note, Joe I put sugar on his tomatoes.

EARLY YEARS

The only home that I remember was 44 Crestwood in Clayton, Missouri. My best friends were the Erkers– especially Buddy.

Buddy and I did our homework together, walked to school together, and played softball and touch football, weather permitting. We also published (typed) a neighborhood newspaper.

Benny May, another neighbor, did not like me. On several occasions he hit me. I got revenge by pulling him off his bike and pushing him into a pile of manure, face down. I also poured ink into his mailbox.

I attended grade school at Our Lady of Lourdes Parish. All the teachers were nuns. I had a great time there except for two instances.

One – I put Limburger cheese on the radiator and the smell drove everyone out of the room.

Two – Because of multiple abscess ear problems and resulting school absences, I flunked 2nd grade. I'll never forget the day that all my friends advanced to 3rd grade and I was told to stay in my seat. I was hurt and deeply humiliated. But in an important way that experience paid off. I said to myself "I'll never fail again." I repeated this pledge when I flunked Military Topography and Graphics during my first year at West Point. On the way down to take a day long "turn out" exam, I said to myself, "I won't fail again." And just before the exam began Col. Walter M. Higgins ("Higgie") said, "Mr. Muckerman here is a one way ticket home. Turn outs are like musical chairs, when the music stops some people don't have a chair and I believe that you will be one of them."

I looked him straight in the eye and said, "Colonel Higgins, the only way that you will get me out of here is feet first."

Two days later I was told that I had passed and went on to my second year at West Point. In retrospect, I believe those strong words saved me. Col. Higgins probably concluded that this cadet was no quitter.

Meantime back to Crestwood and my high school years. I attended St. Louis U. High which was run by the Jesuits. The Jebbies, as they were known, were very tough and I learned a lot during my years there.

Dad drove me to school because it was about 15 miles from our new home in Country Life Acres. Unfortunately he picked me up at 4 o'clock each day and, therefore, I could not participate in the after school sports programs. Instead I worked in the yard and on all and winter weekends I hunted with my best friend Tom Osterling and my Irish Setter, Mike.

One of my neighbors was Branch Rickey, owner of the Cardinals. One day Branch knocked on our door and said that he was going to shoot Mike because he had killed 4 of his ducks and put them on our doorstep (for me). I said, "Mr. Rickey, you can shoot me but not Mike." He backed off.

This is the end of the written narrative.

Published Articles and Letters written by Joseph E. Muckerman, II

Articles

"The Root Cause of Our Iraq Dilemma Is The Inability to Mobilize Industrial Capability"

Manufacturing News, Vol. 14, No. 4, February 23, 2007

"The Defense Technology and Industrial Base: Key Components of National Power"

Written with Gordon Boezer and Ivars Gutmanis.

PARAMETERS, The U. S. Army War College Quarterly, Summer, 1997

"L is for Logistics"

A book review of *The Big 'L': American Logistics in WWII.*

An **Industrial College of the Armed Forces Study, edited by Alan L. Gropman**.

Review appeared in *Joint Force Quarterly*, National Defense University Press, Summer, 1997

"Rethink the Nuclear Threat"

Written with John R. Powers

ORBIS, a Journal of World Affairs of the Foreign Policy Research Institute, Vol. 38, Winter, **1994**

"Mobilization"

Written with James Miskel

National Defense Magazine, Journal of the American Defense Preparedness Association

April, 1989

"A Strategic Rationale for Mobilization",

Written with Ralph Sanders

Strategic Review Magazine, Summer, 1984

"Pearl Harbor Remembered"

An Op-Ed piece —*Washington Times*, December 7, 1982

"Does The Arsenal of Democracy Have a Mobilization Plan?"

Military Review Magazine, May, 1982

"Hedging on a Strategic Gamble"

ARMY Magazine, September, 1971

"Bay of Pigs Revisited"

Military Review Magazine, April, 1971

To the Editor – published letters

The New York Times

February 1, 2004	"Our Marriages, Our Government" To Op-Ed by Laura Kipnis, January 25, 2004, "Should This Marriage Be Saved?", **February 1, 2004**
June 24, 2002	"Pre-emptive Strikes" To Editorial, "Striking First", June 23, 2002
July 12, 2001	"Stay on Guard Against Terrorism" To Larry C. Johnson's, "The Declining Terrorism Threat" **July 10, 2001**
September 6, 2000	"An Army At The Ready" To article "What War Ready Means" **September 4, 2000**
December 16, 1999	"Lesson of Pearl Harbor" To Howard W. French's, "Pearl Harbor Truly A Sneak Attack", **December 9, 1999**
January 24, 1997	"Missile Defense is Still a Bad Idea" To Edward L. Rowny's, "What Will Prevent A Missile Attack?" January 24, 1997

November 16, 1996 "The Basis of our Superpower Status"

To Harry Stonecipher article,

"The Fighters on Which They Bet the Farm",

November 11, 1996

October 8, 1996 "U. S. Ship Subsidies Enhance Global Status"

To article "On Second Thought, U. S. Decides Shipyard Subsidies Aren't So Bad",

October 3, 1996

Washington Post

June 22, 2010 "A Blow for Democracy's Arsenal"

To article "U. S. Buying Heliocopters from Russia; Lawmakers Balk at Pentagon's Purchase",

June 19, 2010

February 23, 2006 "The 'Total Force' and More"

To Melvin Laird op-ed , "Don't Downsize The Guard",

February 6, 2006

December 8, 2001 "Unprepared for the Worst"

To op-ed by David Broder, "It Wasn't Pearl Harbor",

December 5, 2001

January 12, 2000 "Why the Apaches Never Flew in Kosovo"

To article "Risk & Restraint: Why The Apaches Never Flew In Kosovo",

December 29, 1999

February 22, 1997 "Realistic Military Planning"

To op-ed by Sen. Charles Robb, January 15, 1997

To op-ed by Lawrence Korb, January 29, 1997

RATED OFFICER'S NAME, GRADE, SERVICE NUMBER AND SSAN: MUCKERMAN, JOSEPH E., II, COL, 498-44-7596

PART V - DUTY ASSIGNMENT FOR RATED PERIOD (Read paragraph 4-3a, AR 623-105)

a. PRINCIPAL DUTY — b. DUTY MOS 2728 — c. AUTH GRADE COL

Director, Communist Military Strategy Studies, Department of Strategy,

d. MAJOR ADDITIONAL DUTIES Served as Course Adviser in Course 5, entitled "Joint Strategic (Cont)

PART VI - PERFORMANCE OF DUTY FACTORS (Read paragraph 4-3f, AR 623-105)

Scores: TOP 1, SECOND 2, MIDDLE 3, FOURTH 4, BOTTOM 5, NOT OBSERVED N/O

RATER	INDORSER	Factor
1	1	a. DISPLAYS A PROFESSIONAL KNOWLEDGE OF ASSIGNED DUTIES
1	N/O	b. MANAGES RESOURCES EFFICIENTLY AND ECONOMICALLY
1	1	c. ESTABLISHES AND ACHIEVES HIGH STANDARDS OF PERFORMANCE
N/O	N/O	d. FULFILLS HIS RESPONSIBILITIES IN THE DEVELOPMENT OF SUBORDINATES
1	1	e. PLANS BEYOND THE IMMEDIATE REQUIREMENTS OF ASSIGNED DUTIES
1	1	f. DELEGATES AUTHORITY AS APPROPRIATE
1	1	g. EXERCISES PROPER DEGREE OF SUPERVISION
1	1	h. COMMANDS CONFIDENCE AND RESPECT
1	1	i. ACCEPTS FULL RESPONSIBILITY FOR HIS ACTIONS
1	1	j. WILLINGLY ACCEPTS AND ACTS UPON SUGGESTIONS AND CONSTRUCTIVE CRITICISM
1	1	k. EXPRESSES HIMSELF CLEARLY AND CONCISELY ORALLY
1	1	l. EXPRESSES HIMSELF CLEARLY AND CONCISELY IN WRITING
1	1	m. MAINTAINS AN APPROPRIATE LEVEL OF PHYSICAL FITNESS
N/O	N/O	n. HAS CONCERN FOR THE WELFARE OF SUBORDINATES

PART VII - DEMONSTRATED PERFORMANCE OF PRESENT DUTY (Read paragraph 4-3g, AR 623-105)

RATER	INDORSER	
X		PERFORMS THIS DUTY BETTER THAN ANY OTHER OFFICER I KNOW*
	X	PERFORMANCE OF THIS DUTY EQUALED BY VERY FEW OFFICERS
		PERFORMS THIS DUTY BETTER THAN MOST OFFICERS
		PERFORMS THIS DUTY AS WELL AS MOST OFFICERS
		PERFORMANCE OF THIS DUTY MEETS MINIMUM STANDARDS
		PERFORMS THIS DUTY IN AN UNSATISFACTORY MANNER*

PART VIII - PROMOTION POTENTIAL (Read paragraph 4-3h, AR 623-105)

R	I	
X	X	PROMOTE AHEAD OF CONTEMPORARIES (EXHIBITS CHARACTERISTICS WHICH SHOULD BRING HIM TO THE HIGHEST POSITIONS IN THE ARMY.)
		PROMOTE ALONG WITH CONTEMPORARIES
		DO NOT PROMOTE AT THIS TIME*
		DO NOT PROMOTE THIS OFFICER*

PART IX - SCHOOLING POTENTIAL (Read paragraph 4-3i, AR 623-105)

HIGHEST MILITARY SCHOOL COMPLETED: SSC

R	I	
		SENIOR SERVICE COLLEGE AHEAD OF CONTEMPORARIES
		SENIOR SERVICE COLLEGE WITH CONTEMPORARIES
		C&GSC OR EQUIVALENT AHEAD OF CONTEMPORARIES
		C&GSC OR EQUIVALENT WITH CONTEMPORARIES
		NOT RECOMMENDED FOR FURTHER SCHOOLING
	X	NOT APPLICABLE
X		OTHER (Specify below)

RATER Harvard Adv Mgmt Program

INDORSER

PART X - ASSIGNMENT POTENTIAL (Read paragraph 4-3j, AR 623-105)

Scale: 1 2 3 4 5* N/O

R	I	
1	1	POTENTIAL FOR HIGHER LEVEL COMMAND
1	1	POTENTIAL FOR HIGHER LEVEL STAFF

PART XI - COMMENTS (Read paragraph 4-3l, AR 623-105)

a. RATER Soft-spoken, Colonel Muckerman has the force of an atom bomb when he exposes his true self; he is a skillful, determined leader and he always capitalizes on his own best qualities. As a junior officer in his very competitive surroundings at USAWC, he excelled in his demonstrated zeal, in setting the example in improving himself in administrative ability and above all other talents, in his ability to achieve sparklingly outstanding results in the unfamiliar academic environment. Recently promoted and now going immediately to a command, I strongly recommend that he be immediately promoted to Brigadier General, far ahead of his contemporaries. He has such innate mental equipment, talent for organization, attention to detail, flair for (Cont)

b. INDORSER ☐ I AM UNABLE TO EVALUATE THIS OFFICER FOR THE FOLLOWING REASON:

The rater has provided a very fair appraisal of this fine officer. The superb quality of his performance was indicated by the fine manner with which the students received his instruction in the Military Strategy Seminar and the excellent results of the committees which he advised during Courses 5 and 6. I reluctantly agreed to Colonel Muckerman's early departure for a command assignment.

PART XII - OVER-ALL VALUE TO THE SERVICE (Read paragraph 4-3m, AR 623-105)

a. OFFICERS OF THIS GRADE PERFORMING SIMILAR FUNCTIONS I CURRENTLY RATE OR INDORSE

PLACEMENT OF OFFICERS (Enter * in appropriate group)

	TOTAL	BOTTOM 5TH	FOURTH	MIDDLE	SECOND	TOP	RANKING WITHIN OVER-ALL GROUP
RATER	3					3*	X
INDORSER	5					5*	X

b. RANKING OF THIS OFFICER IN COMPARISON WITH ALL ARMY OFFICERS OF THIS GRADE AND BRANCH I KNOW WELL ENOUGH TO RATE

RATER: 97

% 0 10 20 30 40 50 60 70 80 90 100

INDORSER: 100%

November 16, 1996 "The Basis of our Superpower Status"
To Harry Stonecipher article,
"The Fighters on Which They Bet the Farm",
November 11, 1996

October 8, 1996 "U. S. Ship Subsidies Enhance Global Status"
To article "On Second Thought, U. S. Decides Shipyard Subsidies Aren't So Bad",
October 3, 1996

Washington Post

June 22, 2010 "A Blow for Democracy's Arsenal"
To article "U. S. Buying Helicopters from Russia; Lawmakers Balk at Pentagon's Purchase",
June 19, 2010

February 23, 2006 "The 'Total Force' and More"
To Melvin Laird op-ed , "Don't Downsize The Guard",
February 6, 2006

December 8, 2001 "Unprepared for the Worst"
To op-ed by David Broder, "It Wasn't Pearl Harbor",
December 5, 2001

January 12, 2000 "Why the Apaches Never Flew in Kosovo"
To article "Risk & Restraint: Why The Apaches Never Flew In Kosovo",
December 29, 1999

February 22, 1997 "Realistic Military Planning"
To op-ed by Sen. Charles Robb, January 15, 1997
To op-ed by Lawrence Korb, January 29, 1997

ARMY Magazine

March, 2004	"Homeland Security"
	To article by William Hawkens, January, 2004
November, 2001	"The Value of Landpower"
	To General Kroesen's article,
	"Front and Center", August, 2001
September, 1996	"Developing Mobilization Plans"
	To Major General Edward Atkeson's article.
	"The Threat from Washington", July 1996

RATED OFFICER'S NAME, GRADE, SERVICE NUMBER AND SSAN: MUCKERMAN, JOSEPH E., II, COL, 498-44-7596

PART V - DUTY ASSIGNMENT FOR RATED PERIOD (Read paragraph 4-3a, AR 623-105)

a. PRINCIPAL DUTY — b. DUTY MOS 2728 — c. AUTH GRADE COL

Director, Communist Military Strategy Studies, Department of Strategy,

d. MAJOR ADDITIONAL DUTIES Served as Course Adviser in Course 5, entitled "Joint Strategic (Cont)

PART VI - PERFORMANCE OF DUTY FACTORS (Read paragraph 4-3f, AR 623-105)

SCORES: TOP 1, SECOND 2, MIDDLE 3, FOURTH 4, BOTTOM 5, NOT OBSERVED N/O

RATER	INDORSER	FACTOR
1	1	a. DISPLAYS A PROFESSIONAL KNOWLEDGE OF ASSIGNED DUTIES
1	N/O	b. MANAGES RESOURCES EFFICIENTLY AND ECONOMICALLY
1	1	c. ESTABLISHES AND ACHIEVES HIGH STANDARDS OF PERFORMANCE
N/O	N/O	d. FULFILLS HIS RESPONSIBILITIES IN THE DEVELOPMENT OF SUBORDINATES
1	1	e. PLANS BEYOND THE IMMEDIATE REQUIREMENTS OF ASSIGNED DUTIES
1	1	f. DELEGATES AUTHORITY AS APPROPRIATE
1	1	g. EXERCISES PROPER DEGREE OF SUPERVISION
1	1	h. COMMANDS CONFIDENCE AND RESPECT
1	1	i. ACCEPTS FULL RESPONSIBILITY FOR HIS ACTIONS
1	1	j. WILLINGLY ACCEPTS AND ACTS UPON SUGGESTIONS AND CONSTRUCTIVE CRITICISM
1	1	k. EXPRESSES HIMSELF CLEARLY AND CONCISELY ORALLY
1	1	l. EXPRESSES HIMSELF CLEARLY AND CONCISELY IN WRITING
1	1	m. MAINTAINS AN APPROPRIATE LEVEL OF PHYSICAL FITNESS
N/O	N/O	n. HAS CONCERN FOR THE WELFARE OF SUBORDINATES

PART VII - DEMONSTRATED PERFORMANCE OF PRESENT DUTY (Read paragraph 4-3g, AR 623-105)

RATER	INDORSER	
X		PERFORMS THIS DUTY BETTER THAN ANY OTHER OFFICER I KNOW *
	X	PERFORMANCE OF THIS DUTY EQUALED BY VERY FEW OFFICERS
		PERFORMS THIS DUTY BETTER THAN MOST OFFICERS
		PERFORMS THIS DUTY AS WELL AS MOST OFFICERS
		PERFORMANCE OF THIS DUTY MEETS MINIMUM STANDARDS
		PERFORMS THIS DUTY IN AN UNSATISFACTORY MANNER *

PART VIII - PROMOTION POTENTIAL (Read paragraph 4-3h, AR 623-105)

R	I	
X	X	PROMOTE AHEAD OF CONTEMPORARIES (EXHIBITS CHARACTERISTICS WHICH SHOULD BRING HIM TO THE HIGHEST POSITIONS IN THE ARMY.)
		PROMOTE ALONG WITH CONTEMPORARIES
		DO NOT PROMOTE AT THIS TIME*
		DO NOT PROMOTE THIS OFFICER*

PART IX - SCHOOLING POTENTIAL (Read paragraph 4-3i, AR 623-105)

SSC — HIGHEST MILITARY SCHOOL COMPLETED

R	I	
		SENIOR SERVICE COLLEGE AHEAD OF CONTEMPORARIES
		SENIOR SERVICE COLLEGE WITH CONTEMPORARIES
		C&GSC OR EQUIVALENT AHEAD OF CONTEMPORARIES
		C&GSC OR EQUIVALENT WITH CONTEMPORARIES
		NOT RECOMMENDED FOR FURTHER SCHOOLING ASSIGNMENTS
	X	NOT APPLICABLE
X		OTHER (Specify below)

RATER Harvard Adv Mgmt Program

INDORSER

PART X - ASSIGNMENT POTENTIAL (Read paragraph 4-3j, AR 623-105)

R	I	1 2 3 4 5* N/O
1	1	POTENTIAL FOR HIGHER LEVEL COMMAND
1	1	POTENTIAL FOR HIGHER LEVEL STAFF

PART XI - COMMENTS (Read paragraph 4-3l, AR 623-105)

a. RATER Soft-spoken, Colonel Muckerman has the force of an atom bomb when he exposes his true self; he is a skillful, determined leader and he always capitalizes on his own best qualities. As a junior officer in his very competitive surroundings at USAWC, he excelled in his demonstrated zeal, in setting the example in improving himself in administrative ability and above all other talents, in his ability to achieve sparklingly outstanding results in the unfamiliar academic environment. Recently promoted and now going immediately to a command, I strongly recommend that he be immediately promoted to Brigadier General, far ahead of his contemporaries. He has such innate mental equipment, talent for organization, attention to detail, flair for (Cont)

b. INDORSER ☐ I AM UNABLE TO EVALUATE THIS OFFICER FOR THE FOLLOWING REASON: The rater has provided a very fair appraisal of this fine officer. The superb quality of his performance was indicated by the fine manner with which the students received his instruction in the Military Strategy Seminar and the excellent results of the committees which he advised during Courses 5 and 6. I reluctantly agreed to Colonel Muckerman's early departure for a command assignment.

PART XII - OVER-ALL VALUE TO THE SERVICE (Read paragraph 4-3m, AR 623-105)

a. OFFICERS OF THIS GRADE PERFORMING SIMILAR FUNCTIONS I CURRENTLY RATE OR INDORSE — PLACEMENT OF OFFICERS (Enter * in appropriate group)

	TOTAL	BOTTOM 5TH	FOURTH	MIDDLE	SECOND	TOP	RATING OF THE OVER-ALL GROUP
RATER	3					3*	X
INDORSER	5					5*	X

b. RANKING OF THIS OFFICER IN COMPARISON WITH ALL ARMY OFFICERS OF THIS GRADE AND BRANCH I KNOW WELL ENOUGH TO RATE

RATER: 100 (marked at 100%)

% 0 10 20 30 40 50 60 70 80 90 100

INDORSER: 100%